Text on the 1988 Indiana Aeronautical Chart
is as follows:

THE HALSMER BROTHERS

This year's cover pays tribute to the Halsmer Brothers and 60 years of innovation and engineering ingenuity.

Frances, John and Joseph Halsmer built their first planes in 1931 and taught themselves how to fly on their dad's dairy farm. Their first plane operated on a Ford Model T engine, but bounced better than it flew. The brothers later traded 40 bushels of corn for a WWI biplane, and Halsmer's Dairy soon became Halsmer's Airport. While all three Halsmer brothers taught flying, they also performed additional managerial, inspection, and licensing duties.

During WWI the brothers served in the AAF but returned soon after to form Halsmer Flying Service where they continued giving lessons and flying charters. Joseph turned the airport into his personal workshop where he invented the Aero Car, the Halsmer Safety Twin, and a push-pull airplane with fore and aft propellers. He also claimed several records, including one for the fastest turbo-prop trans-Atlantic flight.

Halsmer Airport was the result of a dream of three brothers who became hooked on aviation after a trip to an air show in 1927. Now, 53 years later, the Halsmer Airport will close to make room for further growth and progress in Indiana. Although physically gone, the memory of the airport will remain, and the contributions of the Halsmer Brothers will be seen in aviation history as a significant component in Indiana's aviation development.

INDIANA AERONAUTICAL CHART

Reproduction courtesy of Indiana Department of
Transportation, Division of Aeronautics, Deputy
Commissioner Dennis E. Faulkenberg

CHOSEN TO FLY
A 60-Year LOVE AFFAIR with Aviation— and Beyond

by
Josephine Halsmer

THE APPLE TREE PRESS
1434 South 500 E
Lafayette, IN 47905-8718

CHOSEN TO FLY
A 60-Year LOVE AFFAIR with Aviation—
and Beyond

by Josephine Halsmer

All Scripture quotations are taken from the HOLY BIBLE, NEW INTERNATIONAL VERSION®. Copyright © 1973, 1978, 1984 by International Bible Society. Used by permission of Zondervan Publishing House. All rights reserved.

All photos are the property of THE APPLE TREE PRESS, with these exceptions: photos of Canadair CL-44 and Douglas DC-8, courtesy of Capt. Joseph Szaflarski, Ret. SWA; photos of Halsmer Dairy wagon, Ford engine plane, and the damaged Taperwing, courtesy of Evelyn Halsmer.

Although the author has exhaustively researched all sources to ensure the accuracy and completeness of the information contained herein, no responsibility is assumed for errors, inaccuracies, omissions, or inconsistencies. Any slights of people or organizations are unintentional.

Printed by BookCrafters, Inc.

Cover art by Keith Butz

Book design by Ron Smith, Twin City Typesetting

Publishers Cataloging in Publication Data

Halsmer, Josephine

Chosen to fly: a 60-year love affair with aviation—and beyond/by Josephine Halsmer. 1st ed.

   ISBN 0-9632834-4-8 LCCC 92-71762

1. Halsmer, Joseph L., 1914-
2. Air pilots—United States—Biography.
3. Aeronautics—History.
4. Stunt flying
5. World War, 1939-1945—Personal narratives, American.
6. Christian life. I. Title.

Published by THE APPLE TREE PRESS First Printing 1992

Printed in the United States of America.

DEDICATION

To Mom and Pop—To Mother and Dad
and those who went before them
for standing joyfully and faithfully in the chain of life

and, with a salute,

to our children and grandchildren
and all who follow them.

Let this be written for a future generation,
that a people not yet created may praise the Lord.

Ps. 102:18

PREFACE

Writing this story was not a task I accepted readily. But about the time of the airport sale, there came a strong impression that it was something I SHOULD do. At that time, Joe and I were preparing to go south for our first full winter in the sunshine. A conveniently timed course on "How to Write Your Memoirs," together with help from our daughter's husband, Mike Marsh, on the acquisition and use of a computer encouraged me. We drove south, and two weeks, plus three or four long distance phone calls later, I was pounding away on the keys while Joe retold all those wonderful days.

The complex threads of his life began to weave themselves together into a meaningful piece. The years in which he lived, growing up with aviation as he did, afforded him unique and wonderful opportunities, which he used to fullest advantage.

It has been an exciting time recalling the marvelous things God has done in our lives and it has only nourished and strengthened our gratitude to Him. As Joe often repeated the story of the prophetic vision about his protection in the Stearman, he always included: "... and Jesus handed him a book." For years, neither of us gave much thought to that small detail.

Now it seems significant.

ACKNOWLEDGMENTS

To all those who encouraged and supported me in so many ways as I struggled over giving birth to this book, I am most grateful.

Special mention must go to specific helpers like son-in-love, Michael Marsh, who provided a computer, taught me to use it and stood by at every crisis. Our son, David, gave invaluable advice, time, and support. Special mention also to Marge and Rick Knoth for sharing generously of their time and experience.

Many thanks to Evelyn Halsmer, TV Traffic Coordinator of Purdue University Center for Instructional Service, for research help of all kinds. Thanks to Helen Q. Schroyer, librarian for Purdue University Special Collections, to Barb Stair and Dick McIntyre at the Purdue Aviation Technology Library, as well as to Theresa Clayton, Sharon Kern and Marcia Lytle of the reference staff at Tippecanoe County Public Library for more of the same. I'm grateful to Ann and John Fassnacht and Wally Griffith for additional information about the Gates Flying Circus. Janet and Channing Blickenstaff gave valuable editing help and Kathy Heaphy's copy editing cleaned up my grammar and punctuation. On several occasions, Bill Whelan, Director of Publications at Purdue University, shared generously his experience and counsel. And a thank-you to Bill Gettings, Jim Murtaugh, Bob Mucker, Katie and Charles Mecklenberg, Fred McCarthy, Bob Peterson, and award-winning author, Krista Reed, for their gracious assistance in special matters.

Grateful acknowledgement of constant prayer support and encouragement goes to each of our children, with special hugs for daughters, Marianna Reed, Joann Berte, and Maureen Marsh, who offered untiring listening ears. Thanks also for that same kind of support from many friends, especially Stew and Cec Lindke, Irene Conner and Gale and Georgia Felix, and dear sister-in-love, Louise Halsmer. I've appreciated also the encouragement of Byron Parvis and Bob Kriebel of the Lafayette Journal and Courier.

Most especially, my love and gratitude to my husband for preparing and eating with such well-feigned enjoyment so many microwaved meals.

The Author

CONTENTS

FOREWORD

CHOSEN TO FLY is a man's story of life and flight—according to Joe Halsmer. It could be said—dreams on wings.

It's about dreams that many of us had as young lads at a time when aviation was probably at its highest peak as an inspiration to young men who lived and dreamed airplanes.

Joe's story is somewhat like a diary that will take you through his life as a young man in 1927. Joe was the son of a dairy farmer, familiar with hard work and machinery. When barnstormers landed near their home, his aviation dreams were solidified.

Flying before WW II, he joined the Army Air Corp, serving both in the States and flying the Hump in the China-Burma-India theatre.

The Halsmer Airport in Indiana gave the closeness to the people who loved the pleasures of flight and the closeness of family life.

When the opportunity arrived to put his God-given talents of flight to an even more challenging purpose, Joe went into worldwide airline flying. It provided a livelihood for his growing family.

While flight may have seemed almost a religion to Joe, the focus of his life was sharpened when he came to see that his family and his great faith in people, as well as his flying, were all truly gifts from his God.

You will enjoy Joe's diary-like story that carries you through the life of an aviation enthusiast. Maybe a life such as your own.

Paul H. Poberezny
EAA Founder
Chairman of the Board

CHAPTER 1

SAVED BY A STAR

Terror over the North Atlantic—
growing up on a dairy farm

"**M**ac," the captain shouted, "Put your light on the airspeed dial!" The comfortable familiarity of the cockpit had disappeared in a flood of blackness. In the dense cloud, the reassuring hum of the big air-freighter's four engines continued. But as they cruised along over the North Atlantic at 14,000 feet, westbound for New York, the whole electrical system of this brand new $2 million plane had gone dead.

As the engineer grabbed his flashlight, the co-pilot's voice stopped mid-sentence. The mind of each crewman slipped automatically into emergency mode. In thirty seconds, these instruments would be drained of power and totally useless. Sheltered by the dark, each man fought off his own personal panic.

Mac, his mouth dry, closed his lips, swallowed hard and focused his flashlight on the airspeed instrument. As the co-pilot, Slim, waited silently, a vivid memory of long ago swept over his mind—vertigo! With dread, he remembered all too clearly that eerie sensation of disorientation, that awful feeling of not knowing if one were upside down or rightside up.

Beneath them was nothing but black water. Pressing in all around was the solid impenetrable fog. But somewhere above, the stars offered navigational help.

In a gut reaction, the pilot thrust all four throttles forward for full power, moving them from cruising speed to maximum climb. As he pulled the nose up hard, his short stocky frame pressed against the seat. The burning of the additional fuel was reflected in the slightly deepened roar of the powerful engines.

"Gyro horizon too, Mac", he breathed through gritted teeth, "and the compass."

Every cell in Captain Joe Halsmer's mind and body focused on keeping his heading straight and the wing of his plane level. He knew he could manage to do that as long as these vital instruments remained accurate. With the engineer's flashlight piercing the 2:00 A.M. darkness, he watched his airspeed intently. He was acutely aware of the danger of stalling the plane by aiming its nose upward at such an angle, but they had to get above the fog. Every eye in the cockpit desperately scanned for a star.

In the dim light, the sensitive horizon bar suddenly fluctuated wildly, then became fixed in a meaningless position. Its power was gone. The needle on the airspeed dial faltered, staggered upward and slowly sank to zero. Halsmer's impassive face gave no sign of his concern, but his stomach began to churn.

*   *   *

This crew was manning one of several new turbo-prop Canadairs recently purchased by Seaboard World Airlines. All the Seaboard cockpit personnel had spent six weeks at the factory in Montreal, Canada, learning as much as possible about this CL-44 model. It cruised at 390 miles per hour, carried 66,000 pounds of freight, and featured a radical but excellent design called the swing-tail. The entire rear of the fuselage opened and swung to the side to facilitate cargo loading. Another unusual deviation from the norm was the design of its electrical system. All of its power was furnished by three huge generators with no alternate, or backup, power source. Halsmer had noted this and it puzzled him, but, he figured, he was paid to fly the plane, not evaluate its design.

The outbound leg of this trip had been fast. They had set an unofficial speed record for a turbo-prop plane. Their lapsed time from New York City to Frankfurt, Germany was nine hours and thirty-eight minutes non-stop, a good flight; except, of course, that on one occasion, the lights had flickered. Because this was the plane's maiden flight, the chief pilot of the Canadair company was present, riding in the cockpit.

"What's happening here?" Halsmer had shot a surprised inquiry toward the Canadair man. With a shrug and a non-committal grunt, he had indicated he considered a flicker of the lights nothing to be concerned about.

Now, as the return flight to New York continued westward, Joe reflected on these uncertainties. When they were in cloud, an hour out of Lakenheath, England, the lights had flickered once again.

"What in the world is causing our power to fluctuate like this?" Halsmer had turned to face his cockpit guest. But it was obvious the Canadair man had nothing helpful to offer.

Sitting in the left seat, in command, Joe was fully aware of his own responsibility. His sandy hair showed a few silver threads throughout, but he could easily have passed for thirty-seven instead of forty-seven. In spite of his youthful appearance, his crew knew his steadiness, his calm good judgment, and they trusted him. Crew combinations by the very nature of the scheduling operation were rarely the same from one trip to another. But Joe's forthright, easy-going manner, well-known throughout the line, generally set the tone for his crew, himself and his plane to settle easily into a comfortable team.

On this trip though, Joe's comfort level was being disturbed by his awareness of this questionable safety factor, especially after the second incident. It was one thing to learn in a classroom at a Montreal airport that an aircraft had no backup power system. It was quite a different thing to experience a loss of power while flying in command of that plane over the ocean in deep cloud. He couldn't shake a nagging uneasiness.

He remembered a phrase flyers used in the early days: "There are old pilots, and there are bold pilots, but there are no old, bold pilots."

Joe'd had his bold days, but the several thousand hours he had accumulated in 30 years of flying had not been achieved by ignoring known dangers. His subconscious mind kept gnawing at the thought of this electrical deficiency, much as one's tongue returns to press against a tender tooth. What could have caused the interruption of the power flow?

"Maybe it won't happen again," he hoped. But Joe knew mechanics, and he was a realist. If something could fail once, it could fail again. It was even likely to fail again.

As the '44 had droned along, Joe's hands rested lightly on the unique ram's horn-shaped column. A glance around his cockpit showed instruments packed into every available inch on the panel before him. They continued on around to the sides, even above his head. How very different, he thought, from those early planes he'd flown.

To relieve his concern, he allowed his thoughts to drift back through the years to some of his earliest memories. A grin softened his still youthful face as he remembered the time he stood with his grandfather on their front porch watching an airplane fly low and slow over their farm home. Out past the sturdy young black walnut tree at the corner where his swing hung motionless, the six-year-old stared for as long as it could be seen. How wonderful it must be to float through the sky like that, better than any swing!

*   *   *

Joe's pleasant reminiscing had been ended by the abrupt and total darkening of the Canadair cockpit when he had shouted for the engineer's flashlight.

Now, thirty seconds later, that light showed the instruments completely dead. Gripping the control and leaning forward, the captain stared intently into the fog. In his old Taperwing, his experienced ear monitoring the hum of the engines could have warned him of any faltering that would indicate a danger of stalling. But in this fully automated turbo-prop, even that minimal assistance was lacking. The others waited silently. It was no time for chatter.

Then—there was something— barely discernible. A faint, indistinct point of light shone through the fog.

Halsmer hung the nose of the plane on that single visible star. Was it really a star? It seemed to flicker—and fade. Maybe he had imagined it. Through an interminable sixty seconds or more, they continued to climb steadily upward.

Yes, there it was—brighter now—a star to navigate by!

As they emerged from the fog, the clear white moonlight above shone in dramatic contrast to the darkness they had escaped. As it reflected on the flat topside of the cloud cover below, its beauty deceptively concealed the danger so lately behind them. All around overhead now, stars twinkled like brilliant diamonds scattered over a jeweler's velvet. And standing out brightest of all was the star that had reached out to them.

"I can handle it now, Lord," Joe murmured, more to himself than to anyone else, in the automatic reaction of a lifetime habit.

With the stars to guide them, now the navigator could plot a course. They flew along confident of their position, relieved of the terror of only moments before.

After about twenty minutes, most unexpectedly, the lights flashed on! The remainder of the way back into New York that night, the electrical power functioned properly.

"Don't call me for another trip," Joe warned the Seaboard operations officer, "until you do something to this plane."

Seaboard had been compelled to ground all six of their CL-44s while they frantically tried to learn the source of the problem described in Joe's trip report.[1]

Back home again after that stressful trip, Halsmer returned to the nostalgic mood that had enveloped him before the crisis. In the weeks and months that followed that first sighting of a plane over his house as a six-year-old, Joe had frequently dreamed he could fly. In his dreams, when he moved his arms exactly right, he would rise in the air and land on the barn roof. Then again, doing it exactly a certain way, he would fly from the barn roof over to the silo, and back to the barn roof.

Little did he dream that fifty years later he would fly all around the world from city to city, crossing the Atlantic more than 1,450 times and the Pacific over 350 times. Instead of milking cows and delivering milk, he would log more than 30,000 hours in the air. They were long tiring hours of hard work, but it was work he chose over dairy farming.

Joe's willingness to work hard, and to utilize fully the opportunities that came to him were qualities he received by way of his great-grandparents, Cornelius and Petronella Halsema. When they brought their family to America from the Netherlands in the mid 1800s, they proved they were people not easily intimidated by obstacles. Through their son, Peter, and his son, John, they passed those traits down to their descendants. John (who was taught in school to spell his name "H-a-l-s-m-e-r,") in turn taught his sons, Joe, Johnny, and Hank (Francis), to overcome obstacles and find solutions.

"If you haven't found out how to do something you want done, it's because you haven't tried hard enough," their father constantly reminded them.

On forty acres of good rich Indiana farmland, John and his wife, Rose Metzger, worked hard. They milked twenty to thirty dairy cattle, grew the grain for their feed, and processed and bottled the milk. Daily they delivered it (in the early days with horses) to the doorsteps of their customers in town. It was a family operation and included daughters, Rosemary, Loretta, and Evelyn, as well as the three sons.

Every morning except Sunday, all were up at 4:00 A.M., rain or shine, hot or cold, to begin the day's operation. On Sundays, to allow time to go to Mass, they rose an hour earlier.

Sturdy young Joe and his brothers slept in an upstairs bedroom, where in winter the only heat was that which rose up the stairwell from the first floor. And there wasn't much of that. It was especially cold first thing in the morning, until the fire in the pot-bellied stove in the living room was revived. At night, Pop had carefully banked the fire,

Left to right, the Halsmer brothers, Joe, Johnny, and Hank, ages 10, 7, and 9.

arranging the glowing coals against one side of the firepot and adding pieces to prolong its burning. Then he would pile a full layer of ashes on the top to keep air from the fire and retard the burning. Hopefully it would hold enough glowing embers by morning to ignite the wood as it was added.

Homes were not tightly sealed in those days. Often there was a small drift of snow on the bedroom windowsill. Joe slept with his overalls under the covers and when Pop called in the morning, he'd work his short limbs into the legs. Then, carefully staying under the blankets, he'd wriggle into his shirt. Fully dressed, he'd slide out of bed and head downstairs, where he'd grab his coat and head straight for the barn. The cows provided more warmth at that moment than there was in the cold house.

Summertime was a different story. When the cows were out in the field, Joe would sometimes lie down in the cool wet grass searching for their silhouettes against the horizon. Pensive for such a young lad, he would dream of the wonderful world out there waiting to be conquered. Sometimes he could have fallen asleep right there, but he knew Johnny and Hank would find him and he didn't want to disappoint Pop or keep him waiting.

Those early mornings provided Joe with lifelong treasured memories, as he rode proudly with his Pop in the wagon that carried milk to their customers. The horses ambled along the route in a delightfully synchronized operation. They knew exactly where and when to turn as the father and son toted milk to people's porches and picked up the empty bottles.

In the returned bottles would be ten cents for yesterday's quart, or a nickel for a pint. When times were hard and some empties held no money, Pop always left milk anyway.

"Their kids need it," he'd say.

These acts of warmhearted generosity did not pass unobserved by the impressionable boy. His father's compassion for others as well as his aggressive work pattern was to be strongly reflected in the son's life throughout the years.

After Joe was old enough to be in school, he worked the milk route with Pop until they got to the point nearest to St. Boniface Grade School. There he'd drop off and spend the day. But school was never Joe's favorite place. History and arithmetic weren't so bad, but his most difficult subject was spelling. Once in the third grade, he thought he had finally made some progress. When the teacher gave him the word, "tough", he was so certain that this time he had the correct answer. He confidently spoke out: "tough, t-u-f, tough." How humiliated he was to

John Halsmer in his milk wagon, a familiar sight on Lafayette streets in the early 1920s.

learn that a word that sounded so easy was not spelled the way it sounded at all.

John paid each of his boys ten cents a day for their help around the place. Joe was always planning ahead, and when he was only eight years of age, he had patiently set aside enough dimes to buy himself a new bicycle for $22.50.

He was so proud of that machine. That first day he rode it round and round the barnyard before the envious eyes of his brothers. The youngest boy's tears moved his mother's heart, and Joe was instructed (against his better judgment), to "let Johnny ride it."

Johnny rode it all right. Only he didn't know how to stop it. He was still peddling when he struck, head-on, the side of the barn. Now there were even more tears, as Joe surveyed the bent fork of his shiny new bicycle. Of course, the bike was straightened out and they all rode it for years. But that incident was one of the few tearful memories of a happy childhood.

The Halsmer children also had fun with a pony, Duke, who provided some horsepower for chores around the place. The boys, imagining themselves as cowboys, liked to use Duke to herd the dairy cattle to and from a field across the road from the farm. There was a large pond in this field and it seemed like a good idea to ride the pony through the water. But Duke liked water as much as they did. Each time they got well out into the pond, Duke would lie down. Nothing they could do would induce him to get up. So they'd be forced to climb off and wade out of the pond, to bring home the cows without Duke.

Better suited for other chores around the place, Duke was useful at haying time. In the hay loft there was a system of ropes and pulleys with which forkfuls of hay were lifted and brought into the barn. With a rope fastened to the horn of Duke's saddle, young Joe, astride the pony, was to pull the forklift back into position for the next load.

On one occasion, Joe and Duke galloped enthusiastically away with the trip-rope firmly looped around the saddle horn. But something failed to work properly up above. When Duke and Joe came to the end of the slack in the rope, the taut rope stopped them abruptly, pulling both up off the ground. The horn broke off the saddle, and both boy and pony came down hard. Joe, snapped out of his daydreaming, flew forward over Duke's head and landed unhurt in the dusty barnlot.

The Halsmers were always looking for a solution to some problem or a better way to accomplish a desired result. In the 1920s, long before the advent of the federal rural electrification program, John Halsmer had obtained a Delco light plant from a milk customer who owed him some money. He got a book about electrical wiring, and soon the family

had electric power throughout the house and barns. The outfit generated thirty-two volts of electricity and stored it in sixteen large glass
jars. But it was old and in poor condition. The crankshaft was out of
round and soon a babbitt bearing loosened and caused knocking. (Babbitt is an alloy designed to lessen friction, but it is relatively soft and
tends to lose its shape.) So Joe found a piece of brass from another old
engine around the place. He ground it and filed it until it fit. Now they
had a brass bearing and the operation was able to continue.

When the family had finished a hard day's work, they were ready to
play together. Swimming was a favorite sport, and on hot summer
evenings, Pop would load his family into the car or truck and off to
Kerkhoffs they'd go. This neighbor had a farm on the banks of nearby
Wildcat Creek. Half the fun was getting there. As the neighbors and
cousins boarded the crowded vehicle and space decreased, the level of
noise increased proportionately, but no one complained. When Pop
turned off the gravel road into the dirt lane that ran along the bank of
the creek, everyone's anticipation reached a peak. Under the beautiful
old sycamores and oaks, the car stopped and kids exploded from it like
popped corn from an uncovered skillet.

The cool clear waters of the tiny stream (which could become riotous
and ignore its banks in the spring rainy season, hence the name, Wildcat) drew everyone to his own level of enjoyment. Older boys showed off
their prowess by swinging out over the deepest parts and jumping with
a yell. Waders puttered around off and on the sandbars, overturning
stones to search for "crawdads" or other interesting creatures. On the
edge of the deep water the would-be swimmers tried to sharpen their
skills while avoiding the antics of the roughhousing boys.

On Sunday afternoons they all played baseball. They called themselves the Sycamores, after their road, Sycamore Lane. Joe loved to
pitch and they had some pretty good games. Throughout his life, Joe
called himself a "former pitcher" and bragged about his fastball.

But young Joe's mind was clearly captivated by mechanical things.
He was always scheming of ways to achieve some goal with machinery.
Before long his Pop was relying on him to keep all the farm engines
running. One of his early challenges was his Mom's washing machine.
At one time when she had two old washers, he rigged up a gas engine to
power both simultaneously. Joe liked that a lot better than milking or
shoveling manure, and his skills quickly determined his place in the
family work chain. While the others fed the cows, or cleaned their
udders for milking, or did various other chores, Joe was responsible for
the gas engine that pumped water through the milk cooling system.

There was one necessary daily chore at which everyone took his turn.

That was washing the bottles. It was the most tedious job that Joe ever confronted. First, he tried every way he could to avoid it, but Pop was too sharp to allow that. So after Joe gave it some serious thought, he mechanized it.

He drilled a one-inch hole through the double wall of the milk house directly above the tub inside. On the outside wall, he placed a shelf the proper distance away from the hole for the length of the belt he'd found. On this shelf, he mounted a small one-cylinder, two-cycle Maytag gas engine that he found laying unused in a corner of the barn. Then he pushed a ten inch length of pipe through the hole in the wall, mounted the bottle brush in the pipe, and connected the engine to the pipe by way of the belt and two pulleys. With a couple of washers in the right places, he was in business. Fitting each bottle over the spinning brush was a lot quicker and more fun than hand-washing, and it did a better job.

Joe's knack with engines did not go unnoticed by the nearby farmers, most of whom were more used to horses than machines.

"John, can your boy come over and look at my tractor? It isn't running right," or "I can't get it started."

By the time Joe was twelve years old, he had worked on nearly every tractor in the neighborhood. He understood engines and he could usually manage to make them perform.

But there were always new things to learn. Joe replaced the bearings on an old Samson tractor, removing the oil lines to do so. When he thought it was complete, he asked his brother, Hank, to turn the crankshaft for him while he stayed under the tractor to see if the connecting rods cleared the new oil lines. Joe knew his lip was close to the steering rod, but he didn't know that a spark plug wire was laying on his head. When Hank turned the engine over with the crank, the impulse on the magneto snapped, sending a hot spark through the spark plug wire, and through Joe. When that spark jumped from the steering rod to his lip, Joe exploded out from under that tractor with another degree in "practical electricity".

As in many farm neighborhoods, every fall a threshing ring gathered. In the winter, the same group butchered together. The men brought together all the equipment needed for a faster, more efficient day's work and the families enjoyed the companionship. The women used the occasion to display their cooking skills and the children had a good time with their cousins and friends. But when a helping hand was needed from the children, it was appropriated. In those days, child labor was used without apology and for the children, it was a proud day when he or she was old enough to be entrusted with a message or a tool.

Joe was excited when his Pop said he was big enough to run the threshing machine, sometimes called the separator. This huge, noisy, dusty contraption was the center of attention at harvest time. The wheat had been cut by a binder, possibly days or weeks earlier, depending on the weather, and had been left standing in shocks in the field to dry. On threshing day, wagons went out to bring in the sheaves of wheat.

The men dumped the tight bundles of wheat into the turning knife blades, and as the binding twine was cut, the falling stems scattered and the separating process began. The mix of chopped stems and heads of grain was conveyed into a revolving cylinder where combing prepared it for the shakers.

The grain and chaff fell onto the vibrating rollers over screens that retained the coarse chaff and allowed the fat, nutritious wheat grains to fall into a bin below. From this bin, an auger lifted the grain up into a bucket that held a third of a bushel. This was rigged to dump when full, and it recorded each dump. At the end of the day's work, the men knew exactly how much wheat they had threshed.

Other wagons were used to keep the grain hopper of the separator emptied. The men would back their empty wagons up to the side under the grain spout. It was Joe's job, standing on top the separator, to trip the release of the grain into the wagon. It was a little tricky sometimes for the men to get their horses to back up to this clattering, shaking, huffing and puffing monstrosity, but it was generally managed without problems.

One hot day, scratchy bits of chaff had worked their way into Joe's clothing, sticking to his sweaty body and making him miserable. It was all a familiar part of harvest work.

But he thought, "I'll get down for a few minutes. Maybe I can find a cold drink of water."

So he climbed back over the frame to the small ladder on the side and was making his way down when, for no reason at all, he looked back over his shoulder. The team moving the next wagon into position was out of control. They were bucking and rearing, throwing themselves in all directions as the driver tried to back them toward the grain spout. Suddenly, the strength of both horses became coordinated. The combined push propelled the wagon with full power straight toward the boy on the ladder.

Joe's reaction was immediate. He let go and dropped flat to the ground. The grain wagon banged against the wood over his head so hard, it rebounded and banged again before the horses settled down and held it in place. No one was hurt. No one else even noticed, and the work went on. But that incident was imbedded in Joe's memory. It was the first of many times that a mysterious protection seemed to intervene.

When Joe was thirteen, his Pop bought a nine-passenger Buick. It was a fine family car and with the collapsible jumpseats lowered, it made an excellent delivery vehicle. Pop decided Joe could handle the car well enough to drive his brothers and sisters, and a couple of cousins who lived nearby, to school. Joe was not old enough to have a driver's license, but that didn't seem important until one day he drove down Ferry Street and spotted a police car in the block ahead of him.

Suddenly he became acutely aware of his illegal status. The panicked lad stopped the large touring car in the middle of the block. With cars waiting for him to get out of their way, he turned the car around, jockeyed back and forth, trying to be inconspicuous. That morning, he found a different route to school.

In the middle to late twenties, everyone was experiencing tough times economically, including the hardworking Halsmer family. When a local bank failed, the parents lost what was to them a substantial sum, while Joe grieved over the $3.80 he lost. But throughout the depression, they never went hungry.

One warm morning in May of 1927, as Joe ran up onto a porch on 26th Street with a milk bottle in his hands, the lady of the house opened the door.

"Joe," she said, bursting with excitement, "Lindbergh just landed his plane in Paris!"

"Wow!" thought Joe, "He made it!"

Only two weeks earlier, four airplanes belonging to The Gates Flying Circus had landed in a field near the Halsmer Dairy. That unusual and totally unexpected event had opened a door into an incredible future for young Joe.

He had already begun to build himself a plane!

FOOTNOTE

1.) Investigation showed that a buildup of dry ice crystals on the commutators of the generators had caused the failure.

The cooling operation of the three generators focused cold outside air on the warm commutator, forming ice. As this ice built up on the armature, it isolated the brushes and prevented contact, stopping the flow of electrical current and effectively obstructing the function of the generator.

When the plane pulled up out of the clouds into drier air, no more ice accumulated. In fact, the action of the spring-loaded brushes removed the coating of ice already present and set the instrument free to function again.

CHAPTER 2

"... SOMETHING BETTER THAN SHOVELING COW MANURE"

Building gliders and learning about flying

O f course, it wasn't really an airplane. It was a glider, home made, and still only partially built. But that crude little glider was the first of many vehicles that would take Joe Halsmer through a life filled with challenges, excitement, danger, satisfaction and enjoyment.

Only two weeks before Lindy's record flight, on a Saturday morning, Joe and Hank were splashing away, cleaning milk bottles when they noticed an unfamiliar low hum, steadily increasing in volume. It wasn't their small bottlewashing engine.

"What's that?" Hank asked, and they both stepped outside to look around.

Johnny, finishing up his work in the barn, had heard it too. Now he too stood outside, staring off to the west, but seeing nothing. Then, low in the sky, four airplanes were coming toward them. As the boys watched, speechless, the planes disappeared behind Berlowitz's woods. Then, visible again, they passed over the gravel road and drifted slowly down, landing in the field north of their farm.

"Hurry up! Let's get down there!" Joe voiced the common thought.

The bottles got a quick finish that morning. And the three boys were off down the road.

The four pilots, all wearing high leather boots and wide-top pants that fit their legs tightly below the knee, were out of their planes when the wide-eyed boys arrived. One still had his leather helmet on his head, with the chin strap hanging casually from one side. A pair of goggles was pushed up on his forehead and a long flowing white scarf hung from his neck. With their dark brown leather jackets, and their horseback-riding pants (as the farm boys called them), clearly they were men of a different breed from the farmers in overalls these boys knew.

Soon, a battered old truck pulled up and the pilots welcomed the driver and his companion with back slapping and laughter. The first item they unloaded was an old tent, and three of the men promptly set about erecting it. The others dragged various things from the truck bed. They tossed a large toolbox on the ground and added some parachutes and extra tires. When the tent was up, they hoisted a couple of spare engines off the back of the truck and put them, and all the other equipment, under the protection of its shelter.

Later a touring car and another truck with more supplies arrived, and six more men were added to the group. Some of them were pilots and some mechanics. One was a daredevil wingwalker and one a parachute jumper.

But the planes! They were what fascinated Joe and his brothers. The stiff hard fabric of their fuselages and wings was a blaze of yellow, red, and silver, guaranteed to attract the eye and open the pocketbook of the curious public. They were biplanes, with two sets of struts and a crisscross of wires between the wings on each side of the fuselage. To boys accustomed to heavy tractors, they didn't look very substantial. They could see from the way the men pulled them around by their tails, there was little weight to them.

One, a Standard with a Hisso engine, carried two passengers in the front seat. There were two Jennies and a Canuck, each of which carried only one passenger. In all of them, the pilot flew from the rear seat.

Between shows, curious young Joe investigated closely the tools and the exposed engines in the tent. He was intrigued by the unique valve action of the Curtiss OX-5. It was certainly different from valves he'd seen before. He noticed the wide use of aluminum in the engines in an attempt to lighten them. Most of the many tools he saw were familiar to him, but one strange looking one he later learned was a propeller wrench.

No one paid attention to the three boys as they hung around watching the tinkering and fixing that went on between flights. They had no money and they never got a ride, but every precious moment they could manage they spent there. They never missed the "2:30 P.M. Spectacular Performance" or anything else that happened before or after. The show was spectacular all right, but it never began at 2:30. Right after noon, the pilots started up their machines and sold many people ten minute rides over town. At $5.00 per ride, they made the most money while the people waited for the show to start. (After the first day, the price went down to $2.00, and then later, to $1.00.)

It was scary to see the mechanic turn that prop with a hard swing of his arm and then step quickly back. If the engine didn't start, it was important to be out of the way of the strong kickback the prop might make. And when the engine did catch, no one wanted to be close to that deadly blade as the turning prop picked up speed. The boys also soon learned to be prepared for the blast of propeller wash when the plane turned, but caution didn't dampen their enthusiasm. After the second or third plane's engine was running, the clear summer air was perfumed with the hot oily smell of the exhaust. Joe loved it!

Off across the field a plane would bump along, nearly to the fence in the northwest corner. There it would sit for a moment, the pilot revving up the engine.

"He's listening to the engine to know if it sounds OK," Joe guessed. "Or," he wondered, "is he trying to work up enough nerve to take off?" Everyone knew that flying an airplane was a dangerous business.

Then, turning the plane from side to side, the pilot made sure his path across the field was clear. (His seat in those early planes was too low for him to see straight ahead while he was still on the ground.) With a final push of the throttle, again the engine would roar.

For all the noise, there was no tremendous burst of speed. Instead, there was a clumsiness, an unwieldiness, as the contraption bounced its way slowly down the field. It seemed reluctant to put forth so much effort. But halfway down the strip, or sooner if there was a little breeze, that awkward, bouncing vehicle gently rose and a metamorphosis took place. Now it was in its own domain. No longer subject to the constraints of traveling on the rough surface, it was set free. Up and off it lifted smoothly into the sky.

Soon, the wingwalker went into action. That daredevil crawled all over the plane while it was in the air, climbing from the wing of one plane to the wing of another. He sat on the landing gear, and when the plane came in to land, he hung down and dropped off into the alfalfa ten or fifteen feet below.

And the parachute jumper! He packed his chute into a bag that was fastened to the wing and after entering the cockpit wearing his chute harness, he clipped the harness to the chute. When he was ready, he crawled out of the cockpit and jumped, pulling the chute out of its bag on the wing. If all went well, the chute left the plane without getting snagged on anything.

Joe liked watching the parachutist and the wingwalker, but with every flight he grew in respect and admiration for the men who flew the planes. Each time he watched a plane take off, he was in a state of bliss, picturing himself in that cockpit, maneuvering that fantastic machine as it climbed into the sky. Surely nothing could compare with flying.

He told his brothers, "Here's something better than shoveling cow manure."

After The Gates Flying Circus left Lafayette, the Halsmer boys were never the same. Although they continued to do the work they had always done around the farm, their hearts were elsewhere. All they could think of was flying, and when Lindbergh hit the headlines, they had already begun work on their first model. His success and fame only fueled the fire already flaming brightly in their hearts.

They made a decision to fly, and it never occurred to them that they couldn't do it. They had no money—but there were always scraps of wood, metal, wire, and fabric around a farm. So an engine was expensive? They would begin with a glider.

When they had used all the stakes and lathe pieces they could find, they scraped together enough change to buy some one-by-one wood strips which they cut into longerons and braces. Baling wire strengthened the fuselage and wings and also became the drag and anti-drag wires and turnbuckles. They covered the structure with cattle feed sacks. When they had used all of those they could find, they paid ten cents apiece for flour sacks at the bakery. That summer, Mom's sewing machine took a beating, as the boys shaped pieces for the curve of the wings and the tail.

Joe pulled the material under the needle of her old treadle machine, while encouraging Hank, "Faster, Hank, faster! You can pump faster than that!"

Joe knew that the fabric was supposed to be stiffened and that the Gates pilots had used nitrate dope. But for their first trial model, these impetuous young innovators didn't bother. And their first model never flew anywhere.

A second model was somewhat improved. Now convinced of the necessity of tightening up the fabric, they called on their own experiences with stiffening. Deftly mixing a big batch of flour, cornstarch, and water, they faithfully painted every inch of the fabric-covered wing.

Finally, the glider was ready to be towed with their motorcycle. The starched wing lifted well that first hot day, even getting a foot or two off the ground. Later, however, when the humidity in the air increased, the formerly smooth and taut cover job absorbed moisture and sagged from its own weight. They had learned another lesson.

Joe's former reluctance to have much to do with books and reading gave way to the need to learn more about his new interest. He began to buy and pore over aviation magazines and books, and he learned from one of them the design of a Clark Y Airfoil. The industrious boys built the ribs for their wings from this pattern. They also learned from this source that the center of lift of this airfoil was one-third of the way back from the leading edge of the wing.

When their next fuselage was complete, they set the whole thing on a sawhorse. With it exactly balanced, including the weight of the engine and passenger, they placed the center of lift point on the wing slightly to the rear of the balance point of the fuselage and bolted the wing in place. They found it desirable to have a plane slightly noseheavy. Anytime forward speed might be reduced, a heavy nose will tend to lower itself, thus increasing its airspeed and returning control to the pilot. This manner of balancing either a glider or a plane served them well over many years of building.

When the weather allowed, the Halsmer boys worked on their creation every moment they could manage. They would squeeze moments from lunch break or any other time they could get away from their chores. One afternoon after several runs down the field, Joe decided to pull back harder on the stick to see if the controls worked as they were meant to do. Its quick leap into the air surprised him so, that he reacted with an abrupt push forward on the stick. He found himself plowing into the ground. The precious fuselage was busted up and Joe got a few scratches. They all were angry at the loss of the time and work that had gone into this production, but thrilled that they had achieved some lift. It only made them more determined.

By now, Joe began to think maybe there was more to this fabric treatment than he'd thought. They began saving every penny they could and by the time the fuselage was rebuilt and the wing replaced, there was enough money to buy some nitrate dope. This time they carefully and properly coated the entire covering, clearly a step forward.

A distinct change had come about in the Halsmers' lifestyle. Sunday afternoon baseball had turned into airplane tinkering. Many friends shifted interests right along with them, and they continued to come around and enthusiastically help build, or tow, or rebuild, whatever was appropriate for the day.

Joe, the oldest of the brothers, was always the one to try things first. The occasional small increases achieved in altitude thrilled everyone present. But Joe was more concerned with staying in the air longer. He knew he needed time in the air to learn how to control the movements of this strange machine. Increasing altitude wasn't all that attractive at the moment especially since he still hadn't forgotten his cuts and bruises from a few weeks back.

On the other hand, his friends, watching from the sidelines, tended to get bored, so they were continually calling to him, "Take 'er higher, Joe! Take 'er higher!"

The boys had built a trip release for the towrope on the nose of the glider and now they upgraded the towing vehicle from the motorcycle to the milk truck. With the additional power, Joe decided to please his co-workers and try for a little more altitude. He began making real gains, and once he rose to around 200 feet. He could see Pop below him in the barnyard.

"How small he looks," Joe thought, as he watched him standing next to the silo, looking up. "I've never been this high before," he thought. "I wonder how far I will glide. Can I turn and get back into the field?"

Suddenly, he noticed everything was surprisingly still. The cool breeze no longer gently brushed across his face. His heart skipped a beat as he realized he had stopped moving forward!

If he had learned anything in the weeks of glider experimenting, it was that when he lost forward speed, the nose would fall and he would begin to descend. The pull of the tow rope had gone slack because the tow truck driver had run out of space and stopped at the fence. Joe, engrossed in his altitude and view, was taken by surprise and forgot to trip the rope release. Now the still tethered rope was pulling him down.

He didn't have far to drop, but before he hit the ground, his buddy, Bob Jackson, with great foresight, gave a strong upward yank on the rope, lifting the nose enough so that the glider struck the ground in a flat attitude instead of nose first. Jackson's quick thinking prevented a much more severe crash and more damage was done to Joe's pride than to the plane.

With each glider they built, they had made progress, but Joe was getting impatient with the continued need for a tow. He was anxious to see what he could do with a powered aircraft. He had been faithfully saving every cent he could from his small wages to buy some kind of an engine. Confidently he planned how he would mount it on the glider. After all, these boys knew many things they could do with engines.

They also knew some things they couldn't do. Once, long before flying stole their hearts, they had decided to build a race car. One of the factors they thought important (probably from seeing pictures of race cars) was that it should be low-slung, near to the ground. So with an old Chevy, the first thing they did was turn the differential upside down in order to set the vehicle closer to the ground.

It did that, all right. The only thing they failed to foresee was that their conversion produced one forward speed and three reverse speeds, probably the safest race car ever built.

Now, for his airborne efforts, Joe couldn't bear being without an engine any longer. With the precious funds he'd saved, he bought an old Model T Ford for $10.00.

He took the engine out of the car, sawed the oil pan off behind the number four cylinder, and made a plate under the cylinders to contain the oil. He did away with the flywheel to lessen the weight. Then he put a tractor magneto on one end of the crankshaft, and where the flywheel had been, he intended to mount a propeller. He planed the head a little to increase its compression, and the engine ran like a sewing machine.

At this point they needed a propeller. Again, when they needed something, their first thought was to create it out of whatever was at hand. So they found an eight-inch diameter tree limb and cut a six-foot length of it. The three of them roughed it out and shaped it with a hatchet. They made the hub flat both back and front, to the full eight-inch diameter, using a plane and a drawknife to shape and finish it.

Piercing the center of the hub with a very long nail, they hung the prop to swing free, with the nail ends resting on two level straightedges. Then they shaved off either side of the prop to bring the two ends into balance, shaping the pitch of each blade as well as they could. It was a pretty rough operation, but when they were finished, they had a propeller.

They had constructed a new fuselage for this exciting step forward and they were ready now to place the newly-built wing. They set the prop in place, put gas in the tank, hung the motor on the nose, and with the whole affair balanced on a sawhorse, Joe climbed into the cockpit. Johnny marked the proper position and they bolted the wing on. Now they expected to fly.

The only trouble with the homemade prop was that every time the engine kicked, the prop would split. The boys must have made four or five of these hand-hewn props and each time, the hub split. They tried a bolt across the hub, but that didn't help much. Finally they upgraded their operation by purchasing a two-by-eight plank for shaping. In addition, they bought some plywood and glued it to the front and aft of the hub to strengthen it. This helped, but they still had a very primitive prop.

In the beginning, when the Halsmers had rebuilt a fuselage or a prop, they had tried to build the replacement stronger. This inevitably translated into a heavier structure. As Joe and his brothers saw more commercially-built planes, they recalled how they had noticed the featherlike weight of the Gates' planes. They began to suspect that the truth of the matter was that they needed to learn more about how to fly.

It was 1928. Charlie Shambaugh had opened an airport on the other side of Lafayette, and equipment that had been used in World War I was beginning to circulate around the country. The scarcity of both time and money kept the Halsmers pretty close to home and paying someone for

Early stage of the Ford engine powered plane with its "best prop", with Evelyn Halsmer, age 6.

flight lessons was never considered. To Pop, it was one thing for the boys to use bits and scraps they found around the farm and play at building an airplane. But spending hard-earned cash on something as frivolous as learning to fly was something else. What possible use could a farm boy have for flying?

But more and more persons with an interest in flying became aware of the activity out at Halsmer Dairy and people from all around continued to show up. Some were plane owners, and more were would-be owners. Few had any real experience.

One person who appeared at the farm was a fellow from the west side of town by the name of Frazier. He owned his own plane and had an extra prop he was willing to sell.

The purchase of that was cause for celebration. The boys now had their first commercially-made prop and when they put that on the fuselage with the Model T Ford engine, it made a difference. They still didn't get into the air much, but at least with that improvement, the Ford-powered plane now gave them good taxiing experience.

The field the boys used for a runway was barely long enough for a takeoff run. When Joe approached the fence, all he could do was shut down the power. (None of the early planes had brakes, but they moved so slowly, it usually didn't matter.)

One day Pop suggested, "Joe, if you leave the power on full, I think it'll fly. This time, don't shut it down. If it looks like you aren't going to make it over the fence, we'll run out and grab the wing and get you stopped."

Joe was as anxious as the others to see more progress, so this time he gave it full power and came blasting down the field. And when he passed Pop and his brothers, they simply waved at him. He not only didn't rise over the fence—he struck the dead furrow at the end of the field, and ended upside down in a hog wallow. His Ford engine airplane with its new prop was completely wrecked. Again, Joe's most serious bruises were to his ego.

They rebuilt, and ran many more trials, but that plane never gave them more than some good high bounces.

There were a few occasions on which Joe's teenage mind was briefly occupied by something other than airplanes. The fall he was a senior at Monitor High School, his class held a wiener roast on the bank of nearby Wildcat Creek and Joe let his cousin, Liz, talk him into taking one of her friends to it. Joe's buddy, Bob Jackson, was more interested in girls and had a date, so he too urged Joe to go. They picked up the young ladies in Joe's old roadster and, with Bob and his girl in the rumble seat, they arrived as the crowd gathered.

The evening's fun was only beginning when Joe remembered that an aviation film was being shown that night at the Main Theatre in town. It didn't take him long to interest Bob in it. Everyone else was having a great time and the two boys told themselves the girls were having fun and wouldn't miss them. In the early fall darkness, it was easy to slip back to the parked car and leave.

The next morning Joe's cousin was so furious she refused to speak to him when they met on the school bus. And it was a long time before Jackson's girl made up with him.

That same year, Joe and Jackson had a teacher who appreciated their love of mechanics, and he allowed the two boys to rebuild a motorcycle engine in shop class that winter.

They enjoyed it and worked hard on it. One spring day, when they were ready to start it up, it never occurred to them that they shouldn't do it right there in the basement of the school. To their great satisfaction, the engine roared into life, followed by a tremendous outpouring of black smoke. They had carelessly allowed oil to run down all over the exhaust. The smoke quickly flooded the entire building, and upstairs, someone rang the fire alarm.

No one in the basement even heard that. Their first indication of anything wrong was when someone ran into the smoky room screaming, "Get out, get out! The building's on fire!"

With their firsthand knowledge about the source of all the smoke, the boys were able to calm everyone down. The principal was so relieved to know there was no fire, he let the boys off with a brief scolding.

Joe, now nearly full grown at five foot six, graduated from tiny Monitor High School in 1933. In spite of a lack of preparation in math and language, he enrolled in Purdue University. He was still running the milk route with his dad, which meant getting up at 4:00 every morning. By the time he attended classes all day, and took care of other farm chores in the evening hours, there was little time remaining. After the supper dishes were cleared away, he would spread out his books and begin to study. But try as he might to fix his attention on some assigned subject, his mind kept reverting to the best way to devise or strengthen some detail of his latest flying machine. And before either the lesson or the design was completed, his eyelids would slip and his head would nod. After one semester, Joe dropped out of Purdue. College was one of the few projects in his life he left unfinished.

With schooling out of the picture, Joe got a job in the shipping department of Peerless Wire Goods, Inc. He wired up the boxes of the refrigerator shelving they manufactured and was paid the grand sum of $35.00 a week, good money for the time. Going to work in town every day and meeting new people extended Joe's horizons somewhat. He began to think about his future and to wonder what flying could offer his life.

About two years earlier a gentleman by the name of David Ross had donated some land to Purdue University for use as an airport. Purdue was noted for producing some of the best engineers in the world, and in keeping with this policy of excellence, now planned to offer courses in aviation to its students.

In January, 1934, the university took advantage of the federal assistance program called the Civil Works Administration to build an airport on this donated land. That summer, grading was begun, water lines and boundary and obstacle lights were installed, and a runway was constructed. On September 4, 1934, the Purdue University Airport, the first college airport in the country, opened for business.

The old Shambaugh Airport closed down and Captain Lawrence I. Aretz became the manager of the new university facility. There were several planes at Shambaugh's, and they were all moved over to the university field. Thirty minutes after sundown that evening, their new seventy-five foot rotary beacon was activated, and the lights were turned on for the first time.

Shortly after Joe had begun working for Peerless, they had taken him out of the shipping department and put him to work at running the biggest press in the plant. Not only did he like the increased pay, but it put him on the night shift, which gave him daytime hours free in which to fly or work on planes. That suited Joe fine.

When the university airport opened, he spent a lot of time there. He was hungry to be around planes and had confidence in himself as a mechanic. If he worked there, he figured, he could learn new things in aviation as they came along. So one day Joe walked into the hangar at the Purdue Airport. "Cap" Aretz and a couple of mechanics were standing by a Waco F. They seemed to be irritated about something, but Joe had come to get a job and he walked boldly up to "Cap" and asked him if he had any work for him.

"Who are you?" Aretz growled.

It didn't seem to be the best time to ask for a job, but Joe was determined.

When he told him he was from the dairy across town, Aretz challenged him: "Why don't you find out what's wrong with that engine right there?" and he pointed to the Waco. It had a 125 HP Kinner engine in it, a five-cylinder radial. "We can't get any decent power out of it," he added.

Joe went over and looked at it. He turned the prop, then took the rocker box covers off. He could tell that one of the rocker arms was not actuating fully, and discovered that the push rod inside the housing was bent, the source of their problem.

They hired him on the spot, and though his desire to fly was still unfulfilled, working with real planes every day made Joe a happy young man. His dream was growing closer.

Shortly after Joe began work at Purdue, a man by the name of Fred Disaway flew in, in an OX-5 Robin. Disaway was from Sheldon, Illinois and Joe learned that he had an old World War I airplane, a JND-4. It had been stored in his barn for seven years. When he learned of Joe's interest, they struck a deal. He traded Joe his Jenny for forty bushels of corn. On a Sunday afternoon Disaway delivered the plane to the farm on a truck and picked up the corn.

Finally! Joe had a real airplane of his very own!

That same afternoon, Johnny and Hank and Joe tied the tail of the Jenny to a silo brace and got the engine running. What a sweet sound to their ears. The plane had some fabric missing, but they patched the holes and doped it up. Within a week they were running it up and down the field.

Right away, Joe learned something from his new airplane. On all of their homemade planes, perhaps because of childhood experience with sledding, they had built the rudder control so that a push with the right foot would turn the plane to the left and vice versa. On his new Jenny, a push with his right foot gave Joe a right turn. Now, he had to relearn rudder control. He spent a lot of time running up and down the field, barely getting it off the ground.

Celebrating the acquisition of Joe's first commercially-built plane, the JND-4, a WW I survivor. Left to right, on the wing are Johnny and Joe Halsmer, Bob Jackson, and Hank Halsmer, 1934.

Bob Jackson was Joe's first passenger. Good friend and co-builder on many of the previous models, Bob wanted to ride. But when Joe increased his speed and suddenly they were several feet above the ground, out Bob jumped, sliding along in the alfalfa. A lot of confidence he had in his buddy's flying!

Another friend from Purdue Airport was Bob Kelley, who was attending the university at the time. Bob had learned to fly at Hamilton Field in Cincinnati. One day he came out and, in the Jenny, he gave Joe fifty minutes of dual time, practicing takeoffs and landings. Joe was on his way as a pilot.

One definition of flying is "endless hours of sheer boredom interrupted by moments of stark terror." None of Joe's flying had yet bored him, but he was about to get his first experience of "stark terror."

Purdue Airport had been in operation for several weeks, but their grand opening celebration was set for a September weekend.

It was a little windy that Sunday, but Joe was proud of his new Jenny and anxious to display it. As he flew across the Wabash River valley in that hot puffy air, his plane bounced around considerably. It was a terrifying experience! He breathed a sigh of relief when he got it down in one piece. His airplane got a lot of attention that afternoon, but Joe didn't enjoy the show much. Most of his time he spent gathering his courage to fly back home.

With the increase of flying activity at the dairy farm, it was now becoming known as "Halsmers' airport." Pop let his boys move a couple of fences to provide a strip 1,500 feet long, which gave them a southwest to northeast grass runway. There were some low electric wires on the southwest end, but they were a known factor and bothered no one.

The number of airplane owners in the area continued to increase and now the Halsmer brothers provided a runway, hangar space and maintenance. By the mid-1930s, there was an Aerosport and a Porterfield on the field, each with a LeBlond engine in it. The Aerosport was a two-seat, side-by-side open cockpit biplane, while the Porterfield was a tandem two-seater with the cockpit enclosed. There was also a Lion Cub, a high wing monoplane with tandem seating that used a 37 HP Szekely engine.

Joe's exposure to the planes at Purdue, as well as those on his field, began to bring his ambitions into focus. He'd saved some money from his job at Peerless and was beginning to think about bettering his own flying equipment. The Jenny had been a beautiful sight in his eyes when it arrived on Fred Disaway's truck, but now she seemed a little ragged.

"One day," he thought, "I'll have a really classy plane."

The Jenny, in the Purdue hangar at opening day ceremonies, 1934.

CHAPTER 3

"KEEP YOUR NOSE DOWN IN THE TURNS"

The barnstorming years

Joe's knowledge of planes grew. Now, no longer satisfied simply to own a plane, he began to study exactly what he wanted. He learned that some Jenny owners had significantly improved their plane's performance by shortening the top wing. This produced less drag and consequently, more speed. It sounded like an important improvement to Joe, and he began a determined search for such a modified plane.

In time he learned that a man in Peru, Indiana had a "clipped wing" Jenny fuselage for sale for $28.00. It had been stored for some time in a room above a furniture store, but he was assured its condition was good. So he and his brothers borrowed Pop's milk truck and drove there to get it. Maneuvering the bulky frame down that stairway included some frustrating bumping and scraping, but the boys were enthusiastic about their new plane.

Its fabric was in good condition, so they took the 90 HP OX-5 engine out of their original Jenny and installed it in this fuselage. On weekends, Joe hauled many rides and he was happy with this plane.

Then he ran across a Travel Air for sale for $425. This was one of the nicest flying planes of the day, 40 MPH faster than even the clipped wing Jenny. He couldn't resist it.

Aerodynamic engineering was in its infancy at this time and increased understanding was steadily surfacing. The Jenny had a basic design fault: for proper balance, the weight of the engine should have been farther forward from the center of lift. In an effort to overcome its tail-heaviness, the builder modified the tail design. But this created

another problem, so that a combination of factors made the Jenny tend
to stall easily. The only possible way to recover from this stall was to
use full power and get the nose down without letting either wing drop.
If either wing lowered before enough forward speed was gained, the
plane would enter into a flat spin and recovery was next to impossible.

In contrast, the well-balanced design of the Travel Air was a definite
improvement. The airfoil of its wing had better lifting characteristics
and therefore increased the ratio of speed to drag. It had a smaller wing
area and half as many struts between the upper and lower wing, further

Joe with his second Jenny, the clipped-wing model, 1935.

The Travel Air with, left to right, Hank, Ray Korty, Joe and
Johnny Halsmer, 1937.

reducing drag. Because of all this streamlining, the Travel Air, with its engine identical to that of the Jenny, carried a bigger payload faster, using less gas.

As Joe entered his twenties, he and his brothers spent more and more of their time with their planes. Pop, realizing his sons' interest was not focused on dairy farming, looked for an opportunity to cut back on the long and hard work hours he faced every day. He sold his dairy herd and invested the funds in some beef cattle which required less attention.

With the Travel Air, Joe hauled rides and barnstormed all around Indiana and Illinois at county fairs, making twice as much money as before. Carrying two people in the front seat instead of one, and with the extra space for luggage, it was also well suited to charter work. Because its proportion of aileron to wing area was greater, there was greater aileron control than on the Jenny. That made it stable in the air, an excellent plane for instructing. It also had good handling characteristics on the ground, and was one of the first early planes to have individual wheel brakes.

Engine material of that time was not very good quality and assembly did not include the backup systems that later became routine. If one or another part failed to function, the engine might lose substantial power or quit cold. As a result, early planes had frequent forced landings. Later, for example, when second magnetos were added, engines were more reliable. Joe once set his Travel Air down in a hayfield when his OX-5 engine quit for lack of fuel. The deteriorated hose had buckled, shutting off the fuel supply.

Problems with fuel itself were common then also. The inadequate filters of the day allowed impurities to interrupt the fuel flow and starve the engine. Water in the gas was a frequent problem, and early pilots regularly strained the gas through a chamois trying to eliminate water as they filled their tanks. Gas tanks had a drain at the low point of the tank and pilots routinely bled out water before starting an engine.

One of the first things students were taught at that time was how to glide to a successful landing when the engine quit. More than once when the Jenny's water cooling system began to leak, Joe chose to land rather than subject his engine to overheating. (Later it was found that engines could be satisfactorily air-cooled, eliminating the weight of water for cooling.)

The weeks and months of flying moved by in a haze of contentment for Joe. He was having the time of his life. And even when a weather front moved across the area, or dropping temperatures brought a light drizzle or lowered clouds, Joe still enjoyed himself with his friends. In the old shed, which not long before had been a chicken coop, Joe would build a fire in the pot-bellied stove. It took the chill off the air and gave the fellows a place to warm their hands. Maybe it would clear up enough to fly later. No one wanted to go home. What better place to talk flying?

From his Mom he scrounged an old coffeepot which he filled with water and set on top of the stove to boil. From a can of ground coffee, he poured an uncertain amount into the water. Then he broke open an egg, pouring both yolk and white into the pot. Crushing the shell in his fingers, he added that as well, as he had often watched his Mom do.

"Makes good coffee," she used to say. "The shells help to clear it."

Johnny brought a large ring of bologna from the refrigerator in the kitchen.

"I think there's an old lard can in the milk house," volunteered Hank. They rinsed it out, filled it halfway with water, and made room on top of the stove for that, tossing in the bologna to warm it up a bit.

Joe found an old deck of cards, well-worn from family games around the dining table. He loved to play euchre and was pretty slick at switching a card here and there. Sometimes he'd palm from the table a card already played and use it to his advantage. No one in these games had much money, so they bet with nails taken from the walls. All anyone lost was maybe a little pride. As the cards were dealt, the stories would begin. In that day of frequent forced landings, everyone had his own version, each trying to top the other. Often the true tales were the funniest and most incredible.

One day the owner of the Lion Cub was taking up a rather heavy passenger and had trouble getting up enough speed to get into the air. As he neared the fence at the end of the runway, it was plain he didn't have enough altitude to clear the fence. He tried to turn, risking a ground loop to avoid striking the fence.

Instead of a ground loop, his high speed turned him sideways, still sliding straight toward the fence. When the split landing gear hit the dead furrow at the fence, it flipped the plane up into the air and the plane came down impaled right-side-up on top of the fence post. The post punctured the bottom of the cowling between the fire wall and the engine, holding it securely. There the plane sat, as though mounted for display, with the two men in their seats and the engine still running!

Everyone ran down to the end of the runway, helped them get the engine shut off, and lifted the plane off the post. Damage to the plane was minimal and, luckily, no one was hurt. In later years, Halsmer always wished he could restage that stunt for one of his air shows, but it was unrepeatable.

Joe's beloved Travel Air furnished its share of tales. With its small wing area, it required a longer takeoff run than the Jenny. One day he had difficulty getting airborne at Jasonville, a small town in southern Indiana. In order to fly into the wind, he had to take off toward town. His power was only a fraction of what he expected and he barely made it over the fence at the edge of the field. Committed now to go, he continued on, traveling only rooftop high for three or four blocks over the main street of the town before he finally rose to a safer altitude. When he landed at home he discovered the coil in the single-ignition engine was producing a very weak spark, the cause of his poor power.

Not all the unexpected landings were due to engine failure. The relative inexperience of practically all pilots, combined with the novelty of flying, produced inherent dangers. There was that terrible temptation to communicate with those unfortunate earthbound souls below. What daring flier, recognizing his own, or a friend's home from above, could resist circling in order to call attention to his enviable position up there in the sky?

The specific danger associated with this was the tendency, while directing attention below, to neglect watching both the airspeed and the attitude of the plane in the air. If those light and usually underpowered planes were allowed to nose upward in a turn, airspeed was quickly lost. It was a sure invitation to a stall and consequent tailspin. If your circling began at an altitude of 300 feet or less, you had precious little chance to pull out of a spin. A common expression of good wishes between pilots on taking leave of one another was, "Keep your nose down in the turns!"

One student was ready to solo in an E-2 Cub the Halsmers had recently purchased in Crawfordsville. Joe turned him loose and he taxied to the far end of the field to take off into the wind. As he got into the air, the nose went almost straight up and it looked like he would loop the plane. Then the power went off and the nose came down. When the power came on again, again the nose rose, and this time he made it over to the adjoining field and landed. Joe ran as fast as he could toward him on the ground, but before he could get there, the plane took off. From there he returned and landed at the airport. Out of breath, Joe finally caught up with his student, who told him that when he had pushed the stick forward, it would not lower the nose.

They checked the plane and found a broken elevator cable. He had been controlling the attitude of his plane with the engine power alone.

Joe learned that the former owner of this plane had a friend in Texas who was an FAA inspector. The owner had mailed the plane's papers to the Texan, who had signed for the licensing without ever seeing the plane. After this incident, the Halsmers thoroughly examined their "newly-licensed" plane and found several other items in need of repair.

Through experiences like this one, Joe learned to be skeptical of others' assessment of a plane's condition. It was the beginning of a lifelong habit of careful inspection of every plane he flew.

The airport business had reached the stage where more hangar space was needed. Some planes were kept in a shed, but protection was needed for Hank's Waco 10 and Joe's Travel Air. So, with the help of friends they built a forty-five by sixty-foot addition to their old shed and included a cement floor. Now they had a hangar to be proud of!

With Bob Funkhouser, in his F7 Waco, and Ray Korty and Everett Ryker in their Travel Airs, Joe traveled many miles barnstorming and hauling rides. They went to the county fairs in towns of the surrounding area ranging out sixty or eighty miles from their home. Joe's logbook mentions Kentland, Frankfort, Attica, Pendleton, Crawfordsville, and one day at Brazil, Indiana, he hauled 30 passengers. They were having the time of their lives while earning a respectable income.

Once he and Korty wanted to do a favor for their friend, Mike Craig. Mike had a LeBlond Aerosport and he, in turn, wanted to help out a friend of his in Pendleton who was running for mayor. The present mayor, against whom Mike's friend was running, would not allow his opponent to pass out flyers publicizing his campaign, so Korty and Halsmer agreed to join Mike in flying over the city to drop the flyers from the planes. They understood they were not to land in the area because the reigning mayor might cause trouble.

The planes arrived over Pendleton and the men tossed the flyers out as planned. But as sometimes happened, Korty's Travel Air developed a water leak. They headed away from Pendleton, as far as Korty felt he could fly without severely damaging his engine, and the three planes landed in a field.

From their ever present supply of parts and tools, they quickly replaced the gaskets that had failed and were finishing up the job when they saw a police car coming down the road. For all they knew, he may have been coming to see if they needed help. But they weren't taking any chances. They got off the ground as he came to a stop in the road, effectively avoiding any clash with the local police.

Speaking of clashes with authority, or the potential for such, a word should be said about the beginnings of the regulation of aviation.

In 1926, the Department of Commerce, under the direction of President Herbert Hoover, began to implement the Air Commerce Act Congress had just passed. An Aeronautics Bureau was set up as called for. According to those who introduced the bill, it was, "not so much to regulate as to promote" aviation.[1] Within a year or so a system of licensing pilots was underway.

But it was not an easy matter to bring these free-spirited souls under the bonds of government rules and regulations. After all, these men had been flying for years without any limitations. Among many there was a real reluctance to subject themselves to the scrutiny of some unknown inspector. Usually, they feared, he would be younger and probably had flown less.

"How can he evaluate my experience and skill?" the veteran barnstormer wondered.

Many were defensive about their right to fly and fearful it might be taken away.

At about the same time, the licensing of aircraft was also begun. There was a period of years during which these regulations were enforced in widely varying degree. The first time Joe had to get his Travel Air licensed, he flew it to Louisville.

The inspector there walked around the plane that day and said, "Oh, I guess it'll go for another year, don't you think?"

He was a friendly, soft-hearted man who could appreciate the expense of a comprehensive repair job to an owner. He reminded Joe of his Pop. For all the encouragement and support he gave his sons in their efforts to fly, Pop was never interested in piloting a plane himself, although Joe wanted to teach him.

"Maybe next time," he'd say. "This time I'll just ride."

Mom too wanted to show her support for her boys, so she agreed to go for a ride one day. Joe was elated. He took the cowling off the plane and quickly inspected the engine to make sure that nothing would go wrong.

With Mom in the front seat, he took off, and as he got up about 150 feet, the engine quit. He landed without problems in an adjoining field and no one was hurt. But Pop watched the whole thing from home and got over there so fast, he almost met them when they touched down. He took Mom back home and she never rode in a plane again.

Joe immediately opened up the cowling again and found that the gear that drove the magneto was unsecured, its screws fallen out. Joe could hardly believe he had overlooked such a thing in his preflight checkup. He became even more safety conscious.

Ever on the lookout for a better plane, Joe was pleased when one of his students, a city policeman, liked the Travel Air so well he wanted to buy it. Joe already had its replacement in mind. He had learned about a Woodson with a Wright 420 engine that was for sale in Kohler, Wisconsin. It looked interesting to Joe because the owner also had a banner, and banner towing was a moneymaking proposition.

The banner was a fabric cone about thirty feet long on which letters were painted. As the cone slowly revolved behind the plane, the message could easily be read. The September day Joe brought it home, his log book notes: "bad weather." The trip home took him three hours and forty minutes, and he had to refuel at Chicago.

The Woodson was a little-known but excellent plane for hauling rides and for towing that banner. Its power and its low wing loading enabled it to operate out of small fields, coming in short and getting up quickly.

It was a dandy little plane, but they soon learned it had one bad habit. The engine would quit for no apparent reason. Joe and his brothers all considered themselves good mechanics, but they never discovered the cause of the Woodson's unreliability.

Meanwhile, a fellow from Kokomo, who visited the place now and then, began to covet that versatile Woodson. Jack considered himself a shrewd businessman (Joe thought him cocky), and he wanted to get into the banner towing business that the Halsmers had found so profitable. Also, it would be comparatively easy to add smoke equipment for skywriting. Jack wanted to have that Woodson.

After Joe became well acquainted with its unreliability, he wanted Jack to have it too. It wasn't difficult to make a deal. Joe heard later that when Jack flew it home, he had thirteen forced landings in the thirty miles between Lafayette and Kokomo.

In July of that summer, Joe bought another E-2 Taylor Cub. It had

The little-known Woodson, excellent for banner towing, 1938.

a 37 HP Continental engine in it and only burned two and a half gallons of gas an hour. It was a two-seated (tandem) plane, and because it was so slow moving, it was excellent for instruction work. It was stable and docile, a forgiving plane that allowed the student time to react. It landed at about thirty miles per hour. If a 10 MPH wind was blowing, Joe could stand on the runway and talk to his student as he landed.

Even though Joe was still working full time for Peerless and also doing some mechanic work at Purdue, he was instructing many local people on evenings and weekends, winter and summer.

About this time, he also did some flying with Frank Reimers in his Trimotor Ford. He enjoyed flying the multi-engine plane.

On September 12, 1939, Joe located a Waco Taperwing in Monticello, Iowa, and he went out there and bought it. This was a high-performance plane with a 225 HP J-5 Wright engine in it. (This is the same kind of engine that was in Lindbergh's Ryan when he crossed the Atlantic.) Joe was excited as he flew back to Lafayette. With this plane, he could continue to haul passengers, but he could also skywrite, a much more profitable operation. He set about installing the needed equipment into it.

The design of the J-5 engine was such that the exhaust was collected from the cylinders on both sides of the radial and brought down and

The Waco Taperwing, beloved barnstorming plane of 1939-1941. Joe ready to fly from rear seat with Bob Jackson in front.

dumped beneath the engine. Joe extended the exhaust exits into a common pipe about six inches in diameter. He positioned this pipe under the fuselage and it extended almost all the way to the tail. On the rear of this engine, a pad was available for mounting the pump that moved the smoke oil into the exhaust collector ring. This pump produced seventy-five pounds of pressure and he could switch it on and off from the cockpit.

The smoke oil was a mixture of paraffin and flushing oil. When that oil hit the red-hot exhaust collector, it would pour forth a great roll of white smoke. Since the engine was eliminating all the oxygen from the air with its combustion, the oil couldn't catch fire and burn. It could only smoke. It worked beautifully.

The Waco Taperwing was an easily maneuverable plane and in it, Joe improved his aerobatic skills. After getting the plane properly equipped, he taught himself how to skywrite, and for the first time, he started wearing a parachute.

Now Joe began to think he could make a living at flying, so he left Peerless, quit his job at Purdue, and devoted full time to the demands at their home port. As Pop's use of his land had changed, he allowed the boys to move some fencing and gave them the use of a diagonal strip the full length across the forty acres from northeast to southwest. An interesting note appeared in Joe's log book at that time. Where he had customarily written "home port," now, for the first time, he wrote "Halsmer Airport." The entry was dated November 17, 1939.

Joe, Johnny, and Hank were all busy now, teaching people to fly, using the Taperwing, the E-2 Cub, and Hank's Waco 10.

On one early skywriting job, Joe showed that his spelling had not improved much since grade school days. Though he'd gone to school with the Reifers boys and knew the family well, he misspelled "Reifers Furniture Store," right there over his home town for everyone to see. He tried to convince his friends that his mistake intensified the publicity, but he was not certain they agreed.

All of this flying demanded ongoing maintenance on these planes, a matter of continual work and a constant expense. Instead of dealing with only their own safety standards, they now had to contend regularly with the FAA inspectors, all of whom were not as soft-hearted as the Louisville man. There was the Indianapolis inspector who was so thorough, it was a matter of Joe's pride to try to outwit him. Once when Joe took his Taperwing over there, he knew there were some hairline cracks in the wood adjacent to some of the fittings in the wings.

While Joe was waiting for the inspector to come begin his examination, he dreamed up a little reverse psychology. He opened up the coverings on the wing fittings where there were problems, and left covered the fittings that were in good condition. Sure enough, the suspicious inspector, as Joe had expected, immediately ordered the removal of all the covers that were still in place. He proceeded to study those areas intently with his flashlight, ignoring the ones Joe had previously opened. Grudgingly, he relicensed the plane.

Yet on the whole, authority was winning the running battle with pilots, and in August, 1939, Joe applied for and received his private pilot's license with a commercial rating, #53211. (The commercial rating gave him the privilege of carrying passengers for hire, something he had already been doing for years.)

As summer turned into fall, Korty and Ryker and Joe began thinking of flying their planes south to take advantage of the warmer weather through the winter. It would be an ambitious undertaking for them, but they worked out the details and one bright fall day, Joe was ready to take off. His friends had left earlier and he was to meet them that evening at Union City, Tennessee. Then he remembered a compass on a shelf in the hangar.

"Maybe I should have it," he thought.

He had never bothered with a compass in all his flying around the state. The location of the sun showed him east and west and the network of roads threading back and forth across the countryside had always helped him find north and south. But something nudged him to go back and get that compass. He stuck it into the small baggage

Form 345 (CAA 20-8)
Rev. 12-5-38

UNITED STATES OF AMERICA
CIVIL AERONAUTICS AUTHORITY
WASHINGTON, D. C.

IDENTIFICATION CARD NO. 53211

This identification card issued on **AUGUST 3 1939**
to **JOSEPH L HALSMER**
R R 5
LAFAYETTE INDIANA

accompanies and is a part of Certificate of Competency bearing the same number.

Age **25** *Weight* **155** *Height* **5' 7"**

Color eyes **BLUE**

Aeronautics Authority.

CHIEF, RECORDS DIVISION   SIGNATURE OF HOLDER

Tattered remains of Joe's original pilot's license, 1939.

compartment behind his head and he was on his way.

Everything was fine as he flew along through central Indiana. There were some dark clouds off to the west, but he was covering the miles, looking forward to the fun he would have when he joined his friends that evening.

As he came over the hills of southern Indiana, those clouds, moving eastward, were about to intersect his path. His visibility began to decrease, and soon, rain was peppering down on him. Gusty winds bounced him around.

The Taperwing endured extremely turbulent weather that day. The battered little craft was buffeted with such force that the control surfaces on both the tail and wings jerked the stick violently back and forth instead of the stick controlling them. This became quite a problem. Even with both hands, it was difficult for Joe to hold the plane level.

At his left, on the fuselage wall, was the throttle. It required constant tending. Even normal engine vibration tended to jiggle it toward the closed position. Now the jouncing of the plane in the turbulence aggravated that situation. In his fight to maintain altitude, he certainly couldn't afford to have his power cut off.

While he wedged the throttle open with his left elbow and continued to work at steadying the stick between his legs, he had yet another concern.

He had to keep in visual contact with the ground to hold the plane level and also to navigate. The lowering clouds already had him squeezed against the treetops. But the rain was so heavy that, even though his altitude was only a hundred feet or so, his vision of the ground was almost completely obscured. When he did manage to catch sight of anything below, it was solid tree cover. He could see no roads.

Suddenly he remembered that compass in the compartment behind his head. When the storm hit, he knew he was heading south, but where was he now? Flying south, or east?

"How much have I been blown off course?" he wondered.

Still trying to manage both the throttle and the stick, he reached back over his shoulder. With his knees gripping the stick, and his left shoulder pushing against the throttle, he twisted once more as far as he could and ran his hand around the mostly empty compartment.

"Where is the damned thing?" he fumed.

Impatiently pushing the throttle forward once again, he groped for the heavy square instrument. With his torso contorted like a rubber man, he finally managed to corner the instrument.

His troubles were far from over. Once the compass was in his hand, how could he still the needle? And with everything bouncing so, how true would his reading be?

As he tried to fly straight and level, carefully holding the compass, suddenly the plane dropped in a downdraft. He gasped as he felt leaves brush the belly. Gently, but firmly, he brought the nose up ever so slightly.

"Don't overreact, Joe, " he told himself softly. Almost as suddenly as he had come upon the bad weather, he realized the air was beginning to smooth out a little. He was still aloft and the storm was moving off to the east.

He found he was able now to steady the compass in his right hand while his left held the throttle. He drew a breath of relief and began to study the terrain below. Quickly locating a stream, and railroad tracks, he soon identified some communities. Now with his heading corrected, he was on his way to Tennessee.

It was easy to know he was over Union City when he spotted his friends' Travel Airs parked in a field a little north of the town. They had received a hospitable reception and already set up housekeeping with their tent and a little three-burner kerosene stove. Their tour had begun.

At first, they didn't break any records hauling rides. People came out, but seemed hesitant to ride.

Finally a man said to Joe, "You know, you fellows will do better if you put one of your planes over at the other side of the field and mark it for the colored folks."

This had never occurred to these Hoosiers, but this was the south, so they followed the suggestion and business picked up right away, on both sides of the field.

Their old friend, Bob Jackson, who wished he could have gone along for the whole trip, drove down to give them a good sendoff. The next morning it was so cold his car wouldn't start. Joe tied his Taperwing tail to the front bumper of his car and pulled it to start it. It worked, but the noise of the plane engine was so loud, Joe had trouble knowing when the car engine had started!

After three days in Union City, the team moved on to Milan, Tennessee. The main industry there was a shirt factory, and times were tough. No one there had any money for such foolishness as flying machines.

They didn't do much business but they never forgot the wild storm they weathered at Milan. When they saw it coming, they had tied down their planes. As the low black clouds moved ominously closer, Joe changed his strategy of protection. He untied his plane, dragged it to a nearby ditch and dropped the front wheels into the three-foot trench. This brought the wing down almost on the ground so that no wind could get under it to pick it up and toss it around.

Ray and Everett did the same and later, all were happy they'd taken that precaution. The storm blasted the tent and scattered supplies all over the area, but the planes were safe.

After a couple of slow days in Milan, the men went on to Paris, Tennessee. There they landed in the center of a racetrack in the county fairgrounds. Paris was a busy place, and people there were excited about planes and a chance to go for a ride. They stayed there for three weeks.

One evening after Joe decided it was getting too dark to haul another ride, Ryker chose to make one more trip. There were still people waiting to go up.

"Heck, I'll go around again," said Ryker.

And he did. By the time he got back from his swing over town, his plane could barely be seen up there in the sky.

His friends knew he was having trouble finding the landing spot when he flashed a flashlight over the side of the cockpit. But they had no lights to turn on for him. There was nothing they could do. He kept circling and descending, trying to see enough to get down safely. Finally, he put it down, in the potato patch next to the racetrack.

The men had fun along with the business of flying. One evening when Everett, who was quite bald, had stepped off to the side to get something to eat, Joe painted on the far side of his plane, "Fly with the Bald Eagle." Ryker never saw the words and all afternoon kept wondering why people were calling him the "Bald Eagle."

When they landed at different places, they were always welcomed. Airplanes were so unfamiliar and so fascinating that having plane rides offered from his field made a farmer, at least temporarily, a local celebrity. He was happily compensated for the use of his field with a free ride for himself and his family. Joe would then go into town to talk to business people. At $5.00 per letter, he would try to sell them on advertising their product by skywriting. At Paris, the Esso Oil Company bought some time and Joe wrote ESSO OIL all over the sky one afternoon.

The next day, a local farmer brought four of his farmhands to the fairgrounds to see the planes and pilots. They had been out in the field picking cotton when the big white puffy letters, "ESSO OIL," had appeared. Never having seen anything like that before, these folks thought it might be a sign of the end of the world. Their employer brought them in to show them the source of the strange words in the sky.

Another time, after his smoke performance, Joe was enjoying himself so much, he finished up with a slow roll, not an uncommon way for him to celebrate a completed job. But this time, he neglected to shut off the smoke oil before he turned upside down.

The engine quit firing when the fuel failed to reach it. Ordinarily Joe would get rightside up with the prop still turning, the engine would "catch" again, and all would be well. But as the smoke oil continued flooding into the red-hot exhaust system, the absence of normal combustion action immediately allowed air and unburned oxygen to meet and mix in the engine. There it came into contact with the superheated exhaust system and ignited. A tremendous boom split the smoke pipe the full length of its bottom side.

Fortunately, because the pipe split open on the bottom, the explosion blew outward from the fuselage and the plane did not catch fire as it might well have done. After a day's work to repair the exhaust system, Joe was back in business.

In three weeks in Paris, they had done well. Some days they had hauled only five or six passengers, but on others, as many as thirty.

Korty and Joe always found a Catholic church wherever they were and when Sunday rolled around they would attend Mass. The faith of Joe's early life stayed with him and he lived it wherever he was. At Paris, Tennessee, he went to confession. In a conversation following, the priest asked Joe where his home was. Joe told him, explaining why he was in the area. But the clergyman expressed little respect for Joe's choice of career.

"You'd better go back to Indiana," he said. "You won't do any good down here!"

Moving on to Florida, in Auburndale, and then Coldwater, Winter Haven, and other nearby towns, the three put on shows and hauled rides. Twenty and thirty passengers a day were common, and one day they flew for over six hours. Joe logged forty-five riders that day.

Before the windstorm at Milan, Tenn. Wheels of Joe's Taperwing are in the ditch to protect plane from the wind.

Later the team moved to Tampa where business turned out to be even better. They set up their tent on a long causeway between the main road and Tampa Bay and flew from there for three or four weeks.

On one occasion there Joe had a close brush with tragedy. He took off over the bay with three passengers in the front seat. He had allowed a mother to take her child on her lap, something he didn't usually do, but this child was small. He told himself it would be all right.

As the plane climbed out over the water to about 100 feet, the engine quit. It sounded exactly like it had run out of gas, but Joe had recently filled the tank and knew it couldn't be empty.

As he lowered the nose to retain what little airspeed he had, he looked down toward his left rudder pedal where he could see a valve in the gas line. Sure enough, it had vibrated to the CLOSED position!

He gave a frantic kick at it, as they continued to lose what little altitude they had. That water looked awfully close as Joe pictured with horror three other people in the water with him, including that small child. Within about five feet of the water, the engine coughed into life. Those people probably never knew how close they came to getting wet, or worse.

Interest in the planes at Tampa continued at a high level. One day as Joe came in to land after many successful trips, people were swarming around the two planes on the ground.

"Where in the world do those people expect me to land?" he muttered to himself as he straightened out on his final approach.

They paid no attention to the plane above them.

"Get out of my way! Get off the runway!" he screamed above the roar of the engine. But of course, they couldn't hear. So excited were they in anticipation of their rides, that they were completely unaware of the plane bearing down on them from above.

Joe's gas was low and he knew he couldn't go around again.

"Surely they'll look up any minute now and see me coming," he told himself.

As the engine noise finally caught their attention, some of them began to move aside. But it was too late and not everyone moved fast enough. In order to avoid hitting any people, Joe clipped the wingtip of Korty's plane. The damage to the parked plane was minimal, but Joe's Taperwing had a broken wing spar.

He was disgusted. Rather than try to repair such substantial damage there, he decided to go home. It was March, and he was ready to return north.

They phoned one of their friends, John Skinner, in Indiana and he drove his truck down to help them. They took the wings off the damaged plane and loaded them, with the fuselage, on the truck bed.

Korty decided to return home also, but Ryker wanted to stay longer in Florida. So they also disassembled Korty's plane and added his wings to the truck. Towing his fuselage behind the whole rig, Joe and Korty and Skinner started out. They did well until they reached a tunnel in the mountains of Tennessee.

At the entrance, there seemed to be no problem, so they proceeded. But as they went along, their clearance began to diminish until somewhere, with the end not yet in sight, the top of their rig began to rub against the roof of the tunnel. With traffic behind them, it was an embarrassing predicament. But someone thought of letting all the air out of the tires on the fuselage on the truck bed, and they managed to squeak through.

The rest of the trip was uneventful except for the $28 fine in Kentucky for being overlength. That upset them because it nearly wiped them out financially. They'd not gotten rich barnstorming, but they'd paid their expenses and had fun.

This was the spring of 1940, and Joe's pleasant life of flying was about to be changed considerably as a result of the worldwide political unrest. The Nazi blitzkrieg was driving westward across Europe. While most Americans were hoping they could stay clear of war, military leaders knew many more pilots might be needed, so the national Civilian Pilot Training Program was instituted. Purdue University Airport was selected as one of the first sites and pilot training was begun.

The Civil Aeronautics Administration issued Joe Halsmer a license to instruct, and Purdue University added him to their teaching staff at the airport.

It was a busy time. The work at Purdue was hard but satisfying. Joe flew long hours daily in the primary program. Then after a short refresher course at Detroit for the secondary course, he was certified to begin that work. He also taught advanced acrobatics.

All this was done in a fleet of planes including a Waco UPF-7, a Speedwing J-5 Travel Air, and a Manesco-powered Ryan ST. Joe found them all a joy to fly.

He spent his weekends repairing his Taperwing. And while he waited for his own plane to be ready to fly, he also logged some time with his friend, Frank Reimers, in Frank's Trimotor Ford.

During this time, the CAA sent Joe to a Northeast Airlines instrument school in Boston for six weeks, and when he returned, he added the advanced instrument, advanced cross-country, and navigation courses to his other instructing.

In September, Joe took a three-week leave of absence from Purdue to go to South Bend. The government was expanding the CPT program nationally and Joe was qualified to help train the needed instructors there.

An interesting aspect of Joe's teaching at Purdue had to do with the method he and another instructor, Jack Harrington, devised to check out student pilots for night landings and takeoffs.

The field was not properly lighted for such teaching, having obstacle and boundary lights only. There were no runway lights at that time, and there were no landing lights on the little UPF-7s they were flying. In order to land with such minimal lighting, they set up a rate of descent

Joe's damaged Taperwing at Tampa, Florida.

The plane was disassembled and towed home to Indiana. March, 1940.

with partial power on and let the ship settle slowly until it touched the ground. Once it hit the ground, they knew where they were and could finish the landing with no problems.

Even though he had been doing it himself for some time, and thought nothing of it, Joe was shocked one night when he watched Jack perform this fancy little maneuver. It was hair-raising to see the plane lights come over the end of the field and watch them sink until one heard the plane strike the ground.

One time Joe saw the lights go around in a big circle. The plane had ground looped. But they checked out many student pilots this way without anyone getting hurt, or without ever busting up a single plane.

Soon after Joe began instructing at Purdue, a friend of his introduced him to a young lady who had recently moved to Lafayette from Crawfordsville. She and Joe began dating and spending a lot of time together. One cold sunny Sunday in December, Joe took her out to the Purdue Airport for a ride and to show her the planes he flew.

"This is where we get our weather information," he explained after their ride, as they climbed the stairs to the glass-encased tower room. When they entered, there seemed to be an unnatural quiet in the place. The usual chatter was missing. One man was listening intently to the low drone of the radio.

"What's up?" Joe asked, with a strange feeling of dread. He wasn't sure he wanted to hear the answer.

"Have you had your radio on?" The student lounging against the water cooler didn't wait for an answer. "Japan has bombed Pearl Harbor. We've lost a lot of men and ships. Listen, they're telling more about it now on the radio."

The tale of destruction was hard to believe. The Japanese air attack had caught the American fleet in Pearl Harbor and the planes at Hickam AFB completely by surprise. Even now the bombing and strafing was continuing. After a few minutes of listening, the couple left for home, quiet and somber. Both knew this new development would radically affect their lives—but in what way? And how quickly?

FOOTNOTE

[1] Nick A. Komons, <u>Bonfires to Beacons</u> (Washington, D.C.: U.S. Dept. of Transportation, 1978, p. 91)

CHAPTER 4

WORLD WAR II
AND A WEDDING

*A world to fly in and a wife
to leave behind*

The next morning President Franklin D. Roosevelt declared America
to be at war. The tremendous loss of lives at Pearl Harbor had
shocked the nation and shaken its confidence. For the sake of
those who had been lost and for their own self-respect, the American
people were quickly united in their desire to reconfirm their position of
leadership in the world. The vast changes already taking place elsewhere in the world now struck directly at American lives.

A most significant one had to do with people's occupations. The war
effort quickly became total—if your work wasn't in food production,
medical care, or some other essential, war-related field, you were drafted
into military service.

The position of flight instructor was one of the government's military-
exempt occupations. Joe had been offered a position as an FAA inspector, which also would have been exempt. He briefly considered this, but
he knew his piloting skills were an urgently-needed asset and he wanted
to be directly involved in his country's defense.

The Army was hiring civilian pilots, so Joe applied, and was sent
immediately to Baltimore for evaluation. An Army major, who was a
check pilot, put Joe in the back seat of an AT-6, closed the hood over
him, and climbed into the front seat. The object of the hood was to learn
if Joe could fly "blind," using only the instruments in the plane. There

was a needle and ball, a magnetic compass, airspeed indicator, altimeter, and a tachometer.

The major instructed Joe to take off, fly the standard rectangular pattern around the field, line up with the grass runway, and be ready to land on the fourth leg of the pattern.

Joe had never been in an AT-6 before, but, thanks to his time at Northeast's school in Boston, he knew the instruments. Never one to dodge a challenge, he took off. As he gained enough altitude to begin his turn, he watched the needle and ball closely. He knew that if he held the needle one needle's width to the left of straight ahead he was turning at the rate of three degrees per second. It was simple: in thirty seconds of following that pattern, he would have turned ninety degrees. Proceeding for another thirty seconds in a straight line, he made another ninety-degree turn to the left.

Now, he trusted, he was on the "long leg" of the pattern. Watching his speed closely, he gave it a full minute before he began a third ninety-degree turn to the left. Another thirty second "short leg", one more ninety-degree turn, and, if his calculations were correct, he should be lined up with the runway.

As Joe eased off the throttle, the major slid the hood back from the cockpit and there, right before them, was the runway.

"You're in the Army!" he shouted.

Not quite. Actually, Joe was a civilian working for the Army. In the beginning of the war, the Army decided the quickest way to get the large numbers of pilots needed was to hire them instead of inducting them into the service. They called these men service pilots and required them to attend thirty-day courses in military procedure. They dressed them up in khaki, gave them silver wings with a big "S" in the middle, and tried to make them look military. Those drilling sessions caused a lot of moaning and groaning among the former barnstormers, flight instructors, and airline captains.

These thirty-day wonders got little respect from regular Army people, who liked to call them "snake" pilots, among other things. This hostile attitude grew out of the conflicts that easily flared when a newly-commissioned officer would be assigned to the humbling position of flying co-pilot to a civilian airline captain or barnstormer with many more hours in his logbook. While the rookie was understandably proud of his fine Army training, he lacked the experience that enabled the veteran to handle his plane with confident assurance in almost any circumstance.

At this same time, Johnny and Hank Halsmer also signed on as service pilots. As these changes were taking place in their sons' lives,

Joe's parents bought a house in town and moved out of their farm home. The airport business was leased to friends for the duration of the war.

Joe's first assignment for the Army was to pick up an L-3 Cub at the Piper Aircraft factory in Lockhaven, Pennsylvania, and deliver it to a base in De Ridder, Louisiana. It was also his first experience of flying over those swamps and bayous, where any clearing suitable for a forced landing was conspicuously absent. This Hoosier watched his gas gauge carefully as his mind swarmed with thoughts of snakes and gators.

Joe was checked out at the Martin factory in Baltimore, soon after that first flight, in the country's newest bomber, the twin engine Martin B-26.

This was his first opportunity to fly a tricycle gear plane. It was also the heaviest and fastest plane he had yet flown. With its two engines producing 4,000 horsepower, the B-26 cruised at over 200 MPH and its wing loading was sixty-four pounds per square foot. (The wing loading figure denotes the ratio of the total weight of the plane to the square footage of wing area.) By contrast, the wing loading of Joe's Travel Air was eight pounds per square foot. Later B-26 models were built with longer wings. That change enabled the plane to land and take off on shorter runways with the same power plant. This plane cruised 175 MPH faster than the Travel Air and it touched the ground at seventy-five MPH faster. Its speed at first caused Joe difficulty in keeping track of his position on his map as he flew cross-country in it.

It had feathering props, which means that if an engine were to stop or be shut down in flight, the pilot could hit the feathering button and immediately the pitch of the prop would adjust to the point of minimum drag, an excellent safety feature.

Because of its nose wheel configuration, the landing and ground handling capabilities of this plane were greatly improved over that of the early tail draggers. It was a fine plane.

An old barnstormer friend told Joe about his first flight in charge of one of these hot B-26s shortly after he'd been checked out in the plane. He was saddled with a green young second lieutenant for co-pilot.

"Have you finished the check list?" the barnstormer asked the lieutenant. They were already underway.

"Yes," his young co-pilot responded.

"Sure you got everything done?"

Impatiently the younger man assured him. By this time they were climbing out and gaining altitude. The oldtimer knew from the feel of the plane that his speed and climb were okay, but there was one missing factor he had to know sooner or later.

"Well, now that you have time to tell me, where's the damn airspeed

Lt. Joseph L. Halsmer, USAAC, July, 1942.

indicator on the instrument panel?"

Joe's new job wasn't the only change in his life. He and his sweetheart had talked of marriage. Now the war atmosphere prodded them to firm up their plans. Joe presented her with a diamond ring for Christmas and they chose September, 1942 as their wedding date. But they had to be flexible as the war took ever more control over people's lives. All would depend upon Army orders.

When the Baltimore training was completed, Joe was transferred to Trans World Airline's Multi-engine School in Albuquerque, New Mexico. Joe thought New Mexico was a long way to go without his sweetheart, so the wedding date was moved up.

On May 9, 1942, Josephine McCarthy and Joseph Halsmer were married in St. Boniface Church in Lafayette and left immediately for Albuquerque. Joe couldn't have been happier. He had a beloved wife at his side, and in the days to come, he would be flying bigger and better planes than he had ever imagined!

TWA ran an excellent school in Albuquerque. They taught high altitude flying, the use of oxygen, advanced instrument flying, radio and celestial navigation, and how to handle the B-17s and the B-24s in the thin air of 36,000 feet. Joe enjoyed it all immensely.

Finished in four weeks at Albuquerque, the Halsmers spent three short weeks in Wilmington, Delaware before new orders sent them to Romulus Air Force Base just west of Detroit.

By this time, the Army found that it couldn't afford the luxury of dealing with large numbers of its pilots as civilians. They needed to get everyone under military orders. Now the service pilots realized that those drilling sessions and Army courses that had caused such moans and groans were preparation for induction. On July 4, 1942, Joe was commissioned a second lieutenant in the Army Air Force and assigned by the Army to the 3rd Ferrying Group of the Air Transport Command.

The work of the Ferry Command was to move large numbers of new planes from the manufacturers to wherever they were needed by the military. A system was set up to ferry pilots around the country. Officially named Military Air Transport System, MATS, the pilots called it "SNAFU AIRLINE," after a phrase in vogue at the time: "Situation Normal, All Fouled Up."

In the early months of 1942, people looked for humor wherever they could find it. It was a bleak time of desperate holding action. General Douglas MacArthur had been chased out of the Philippines, and many men were being lost in fierce battles in the South Pacific. America had not yet achieved an offensive position.

In his early days at Romulus, Joe flew several different planes: A-20s,

SNAFU pilots, Capt. Frank P. Skillen, Lt. Ben Oakes, Lt. Halsmer, and Capt. John Kenwood, 1942.

P-38s and P-40s, delivering·them to various spots around the country. Later, he was checked out in the Lockheed Lodestar C-60 and spent a lot of time flying the SNAFU line, picking up groups of pilots here and there and returning them to Romulus. The DC-3 and its military version, the C-47, were also used for this purpose.

On one trip from Newark, heading back to Detroit with a load of tired pilots aboard, Joe's plane was "buzzed" by some "hot shot" pilot. This was particularly galling to his passengers, all pilots who would rather be flying (and doing their own buzzing!) than riding. So before the incident could be repeated, Joe rummaged around in his papers and found what he was looking for: a small placard with four stars on it to be displayed in the windshield whenever an officer of general rank was aboard. Joe placed it in a prominent position in the cockpit window and when their high-spirited friend returned, he veered away quickly. That was the last they saw of him.

During those long hours in the cockpit, Joe's mind was always full of ideas for improving the airplanes he was flying. It seemed to him that fuselages needed much more streamlining. The delta, or triangle, wing intrigued him.

"If we could increase the square footage of the wing, which is the lifting area of a plane, in proportion to the fuselage to be lifted, performance could be improved," he figured.

But as long as he lived in Michigan, away from his home shop and tools, there was little he could do except think about it. Finally one evening in their little apartment, he could stand it no longer. He whittled away at a couple of blocks of wood, ending up with a small but identifiable delta wing model mounted on a two by six-inch block.

"Someday they'll be building planes like this," he told his wife.

The long spring of 1942, with all its depressing headlines, had turned into summer. Certain foods were rationed, such as meat and sugar, as well as gas, tires, and other items. But the wives of the military personnel were able to do their grocery shopping at a commissary on the field, so daily life for the Halsmers was nearly normal.

In spite of tight housing at Romulus AFB, Joe and Josephine had found an upstairs apartment in Belleville, a small town on a beautiful manmade lake west of the field. There were several other military families living in the Belleville area. All plucked from their home communities and set down in an unfamiliar place by the common bond of war, they turned to one another for the family support they'd left behind. The Halsmers were now expecting their first child and the presence of these new friends meant a lot. Henry and Doris Renninger and their daughter, five-year-old Charlene, lived in a cottage on the lakeshore and their home became almost a headquarters for the group. Through 1942 and most of 1943 these warm-hearted and hospitable Virginians hosted swimming parties and cookouts that helped everyone make it through those troublesome times.

In January, 1943, Josephine went to her parents' home in Lafayette to await the birth of their child, and on February 8, Joseph Lawrence, Jr. arrived.

The shrill ring of the telephone woke Johnny Halsmer in his hotel room in North Dakota where he had a layover on one of his trips for SNAFU AIRLINES.

"Lt. Halsmer?"

"Yeah, this is Johnny. What do you want?"

"You have a son!"

"A son? Not me! You've got the wrong Halsmer. See if you can find Joe. I think he's the one you're looking for." And Johnny grinned to himself as he rolled over and went back to sleep. "I guess I found out about Joe's new boy before he did!"

When he was six weeks old, Joe, Jr. and his mother returned to Belleville, to resume normal home life. Strange how the business of making war can come to seem "normal", but when the men were off-duty, the war seemed remote. The day-to-day delivery of planes and pilots was mostly routine. Nevertheless, on occasion the hazardous aspect of the job made itself known.

That same summer, Joe was assigned as captain on one of the first Boeing B-17s to be sent to England to assist the British in the bombing of Europe. The flight contained thirteen planes and the destination was Prestwick, Scotland. Joe's crew consisted of a co-pilot, navigator, radio operator, and flight engineer. The departure from Romulus was uneventful, but it was very cold when they landed for fuel at Presque Isle, Maine.

These B-l7s were equipped with the newest and most highly-developed device for precision bombing, the Norden bombsight. Guarding it was important, so the commander of the base ordered two of the crew to stay with the plane all night. Secrecy and protection were necessary, but the flying crew certainly needed its night's rest. It should have been the job of the base personnel to do guard duty, but the crew obeyed its orders.

The next day the flight made it to Goose Bay, Labrador, using dead reckoning (finding one's position by estimate based on speed and time on a course rather than on astronomical observations), together with the help of the Automatic Direction Finder (ADF). This instrument uses directional loop antenna and a non-directional sense antenna to locate a radio station. The direction is shown on an instrument that looks like the dial of a compass, with zero degrees representing the nose of the aircraft, rather than north. The needle on the ADF indicator shows the pilot the number of degrees between the nose of the aircraft and a line to the radio station that is being received.

After they topped off their fuel tanks at Goose Bay, they were able to talk this base officer into providing a guard, so the whole crew got about four hours sleep. Departing at 2:00 in the morning, they climbed to 15,000 feet, and after being out for two hours they encountered engine ice.

The presence of ice affected the fuel mixture in the combustion chambers, resulting in excessive gas use and reduced power. The spark plugs were becoming fouled and black smoke rolled out of the exhaust. To overcome the ice in the induction system, Joe raised the turbo boost of the supercharger about seven inches of manifold pressure. This increased the heat enough, with the inner cooler shutters closed, to melt the ice. It was a very slow procedure, but it worked. They fought these icing conditions for most of the trip.

With the help of the ADF, they arrived at BW1 (a radio transmitter at the entrance to a fjord on the southern tip of Greenland). This, their destination for refueling, was the American military base that lay at the base of a mountain at the far end of the fjord. Although they had located the field with instruments, it was necessary to reduce altitude and get visual contact with the ground in order to land.

The landing strip not only ran alongside the fjord, which cut deeply into the hilly terrain, it also rose at a fifteen-degree incline and headed straight toward the mountains. Landing would not be too difficult since the plane would be heading directly into the wind. But facing a mountain squarely at the end of the runway certainly eliminated much choice about a decision to go around again for a second approach. All takeoffs were done in the opposite direction, downhill toward the ocean.

"The route in to the field is outlined adequately on the map provided, but can only be followed in contact conditions," Joe wrote on his trip report.

It was fifteen degrees below zero when they landed, and all were extremely tired. The wind blew so hard that small rocks constantly bombarded the landing gear struts and the crew wrapped them to protect them from damage.

"The food and service were good, but once again we had to provide a guard for the ship," noted Joe's report.

After rotating guard duty on the bombsight all night long, no one was rested.

"If the Germans can get up this fjord and find the Norden bombsight, they deserve to have it!" Joe was half serious.

Arrival at Meeks was a normal landing procedure, but before they left there, the situation began to deteriorate. Outside the weather office, Joe overheard the base commanding officer arguing with the weather officer about whether or not these planes should proceed. The weather officer was insisting that conditions were too dangerous.

But the CO prevailed, and, flying through winds up to 100 knots, the three of the original thirteen planes that were at Meeks at the time took off. The cloud cover was dense as high as 12,000 feet all the way to Prestwick, and at every altitude above 3,000 feet, they encountered ice. It tore the sense antenna off Joe's plane, destroying the automatic function of the ADF. They were reduced to using the manual loop antenna.

Because of the wartime radio blackout, there was no way to get updated wind conditions. (Neither was there radio contact between the planes that had left Romulus together, so no attempt had been made to fly as a group.) At one point, Joe reduced his altitude to 500 feet above the waves to allow use of the drift indicator.

This is an instrument which enabled the navigator to take readings off the whitecaps and relate those readings to the heading he was flying.

With this essential information, he could determine his true airspeed as well as his wind drift. The pilot needed this information to maintain a correct heading.

Prestwick, Scotland had a powerful range station and it became a lifesaver for this flight. Its radio call letters could be heard for more than 100 miles out as it continuously identified itself in Morse code.

A range station consists of four radio beams centered over an airport and stretching out for thirty to sixty miles in all four directions. Generally, these are set up with at least one of these radio "legs" aligned with a runway or toward the heaviest traffic area.

The four quadrants between these legs are identified on pilots' charts. The north quadrant is specified "N," east is "A," south is "N," and west is another "A."

If you were to fly directly down any leg, you would hear a continuous radio signal in your ear: the merging of the "A" (dot,dash) and "N" (dash,dot) signals. If you veer off to the right, you would hear either an "A" or an "N." The signal you heard on either side of the leg would locate you—tell you which quadrant you were in. Returning to the merged signal allows you to follow the leg in to the airport.

Joe had been listening carefully for Prestwick's signal, and when he could barely hear the faint call, he identified it as an "A." As he continued to monitor the signal, he realized it was beginning to fade in volume.

Ordinarily, coming from Meeks, they should be approaching Prestwick from the northwest. The fading "A" he was hearing indicated he must be in the west quadrant passing west of the station instead of approaching it from the north, as he'd expected.

So he made a ninety-degree left turn and, in time, intercepted and crossed a leg. Another ninety-degree turn to the right returned him to the leg. He could then identify it as the NW leg, because the "N" quadrant was on his left and the "A" on his right. Now, with the signal continuing to strengthen, Joe was satisfied that he was indeed homing in on Prestwick. Oldtimers call that technique a "fade ninety" approach.

As the flight neared the field, the weather became even worse, with rain at the lower altitudes. But by this time, Prestwick picked them up on its radio and accurately located them. The station gave the navigator a heading and brought the plane in on their 6,000-foot runway. It was an exhausted, but relieved crew that stepped from that plane.

The trip that should have been completed in just under five hours took nearly eight. Of the thirteen planes that left Detroit, only three landed at Prestwick. The remaining ones set down in various spots all over Ireland, Scotland, and Wales. Fortunately no lives were lost and the crews returned home.

As the war situation demanded, the men were moved around as needed. Ford had begun building the B-24 at the Willow Run Airport in Wayne County northwest of Detroit, and for a time Joe was assigned to check out B-24 pilots. He did this transitional training at Selfridge Field in northeast Detroit where the runway was longer.

Once Joe was asked to help mechanics move a Lockheed Lodestar C-60 out of the maintenance hangar. It had just had a 100-hour check, including a gear retraction check. He entered the cockpit to control the steering of the plane as the men under the wings pushed on the struts, wheels, the trailing edge of the wing, wherever they could get some leverage. No engines were running, so in order to use the brakes as needed, Joe began to pump the hydraulic hand pump to get brake pressure.

Immediately he heard a distinct "click." Something was wrong with the landing gear! All he could think of was those men beneath the plane.

The crew of one of the first B-17's delivered to England, 1942. Rear, Pilot Lt. Halsmer, Co-pilot Francis R. (Bob) Warner, Navigator William M. Murphy, Radio operator James M. VanSweden, Flight Engineer Walter D. Snow.

"Get out from under the airplane! Get away, Get away," he yelled at the top of his voice!

Even as he called out, he saw the gear handle was in the UP position! As he moved it into DOWN and heard it click into the locked position, he breathed a sigh of relief. What a close call for the men under that plane, not to mention the embarrassment to Joe, if that big ship had settled down on her belly while he was in the cockpit.

Who knows how the gear lever happened to be left up? The only reason the plane hadn't settled down earlier was the lack of hydraulic pressure to energize it. As soon as Joe began to supply that pressure, it could have collapsed quickly.

Carelessness or negligence about locking the landing gear in position could easily have cost a life or caused injury. Joe always considered attention to details and careful maintenance of equipment excellent insurance against accidents.

In the summer of 1943, Joe became interested in work that was being done in the field of gas turbine engines, especially for use in collaboration with the principle of jet propulsion. As engineers developed metals that could withstand the extreme heat generated in the combustion chamber, the gas turbine became more practical.

About this time the German Army was sending their V-1 missiles, notorious for their extremely loud whine, across the English channel. Joe believed that the designers of our early jet engines were losing efficiency in their compressor section. The V-1 was a pulse jet, and by eliminating the compressor section, a pulse jet would improve the amount of usable power available from the turbine. Again, his resources were limited, but he built a small working model to satisfy his curiosity. The pulse jet available at that time was not as reliable as later ones, and he had limited time to work on the project, but he was satisfied that his idea was a good one. When he started up his little experimental model, the whine made his neighbors think the Germans were attacking!

Dreaming away in a cockpit hour after hour, Joe often planned how he could marry the auto and the airplane. It would be a most desirable machine, he thought. Since the wing of a plane is what lifts it into the air as it is pulled forward by an engine, Joe thought this lifting feature should be incorporated into the passenger carrying cabin itself. Perhaps a delta wing configuration like the small wooden model he had carved months before would succeed. Maybe some day he would be able to build this. Ideas for its construction continually filled his mind.

Often as he flew along, he thought too about the shortcomings of the present design of a twin-engine airplane. Granted, for the sake of balance, it seems to makes sense to place an engine out on each wing.

But if one engine fails, not only is the power reduced by half, the problem is compounded by extreme imbalance.

There must be some way of coordinating the operation of two engines closer together. What are the options? One behind the other—one above the other? There must be a better way. He yearned for time and a place to work on this idea.

In August, 1943, Joe got his captain's bars and about the same time, the overseas rumors began to circulate.

Within the next eight to ten weeks, large numbers of pilots were moved out of Romulus to various sectors of the war so Joe knew his turn was coming. A second child was due in March, so, if Joe was sent overseas, Josephine would return to her parents' home.

Sure enough, on November 24, Joe was relieved of duty at the 3rd Ferrying Group at Romulus. They packed their things, gave up their apartment, and spent those extra days getting home for Christmas.

Joe's orders read for him to report on January 16, 1944 to Station 20, Caribbean Wing ATC, Floridian Hotel, Miami Beach, Florida. But the Army wasn't sending Joe to Florida for the winter. They had something different in mind.

CHAPTER 5

FLYING "THE ALUMINUM TRAIL"

Hazardous Himalayan weather in CBI theater of WW II

Within a couple of days of his arrival in Miami, Joe was en route to the China-Burma-India theatre of operations. This was the joint effort of the Allies to contain Japan on the western front.

In Yunnan Province, unconquered Chinese forces were still battling the Japanese. A vital part of the total war effort was maintaining a supply line from northern India across Burma to these Chinese. Also important was supplying the gasoline needed to extend the range of the American B-29 bombers coming from the Mariana Islands to strike at Japanese-held bases.

A land supply route over the great Himalayan Mountains between India and China had long existed. It had been developed by the spice and tea traders in the days of Genghis Khan. In June, 1942 the Japanese had seized the Burmese section of this primitive road and cut the supply line to China.

Ground forces worked from both directions to reopen the road, but this was wild country and it was August, 1944 before that job was completed. Meanwhile, the Japanese break in the Burma Road resulted in the forced airlift of all supplies over these awesome mountains, familiarly called "the Hump."

Joe's first stop on his way to India was Accra, an important port on the west coast of Africa. When they arrived there, he was suffering from a bad case of athlete's foot. With blood in his shoes, he reported to the medical officer, who promptly ordered him off the plane. The doctor told Joe to get out on the beach and let the sun and sand heal him.

What a beach! The Atlantic had been beating away on this sand long enough to get its beach-making skills down pat. The shore stretched for miles, gently curving, smooth and creamy white, with a gradual slope from the edge of the treeline down to the water. Joe loved the water but his baby-fair skin would never survive that African sun. For two days, he made occasional excursions into the water, but mostly, he sat back under the trees and watched the constant activity.

This was not a playground of the rich as such a place might be in other parts of the world. Instead of watching beautiful girls tanning themselves first on one side then the other, Joe watched a group of African men, women, and children get their "daily bread" from the sea.

Using a couple of dugout canoes, each day they took a large net out into the ocean. The net itself was probably 1,000 feet long, with floats along the top edge and ropes attached to each end. As they took it out, the canoes moved apart to extend the net completely. Then, about 500 feet out, the crew released their grasp on the net and brought their ropes back to shore.

When the canoes beached, the fishermen jumped out and pulled the ropes forward with a constant tension. As they moved the net into shallow water, it revealed an enormous mass of jumping, flopping fish of all sizes, each fighting for that last bit of life-sustaining water.

With the net ashore, a general battle began as everyone tried to grab any fish he or she could reach. With no regard for age, size, or sex, fish and fists were slung about like clubs as the division of the catch proceeded.

For three days Joe watched this slice of African life played out on the beautiful white sand, while nature did her healing work on his feet. Soon, by way of Massawa, in Ethiopia, and Solala, on the southern coast of the Arabian peninsula, his passage was resumed. In two days they reached Karachi, an important seaport at the mouth of the Indus River in India. (In 1947, Pakistan became an independant dominion in the Commonwealth of Nations and Karachi was named its capital.)

"Hurry up and wait" is an old Army saying, and it was true then. For four weeks in Karachi, Joe waited for an assignment. For two of those weeks, he piloted some local feeder lines to Delhi, India and other nearby spots. Finally, the Army assigned him to Gaya, India.

When he reached there, he received word that his second son, Peter, had been born on March 3, 1944. That news reminded him how very far from home he had traveled. The long exhausting hours of travel, punctuated by brief glimpses of different cultures, together with the dramatic climate changes, all combined to strike him with the force of a physical blow. His family was indeed on the other side of the world. Young Pete would be seventeen months old before his father would see him.

At Gaya, Joe had truly entered the war zone, where there was an air of urgency not known in the states. Getting supplies into China had become top priority in April, 1942 when ten borrowed C-47s (from the African war sector) flew 30,000 gallons of gasoline into western China.

A surprise attack on Tokyo was planned and this fuel was needed for the planes which would continue into western China after dropping their bombs. Lt. Colonel James H. Doolittle led a flight of sixteen B-25s (normally a land-based plane) off the deck of the U.S. Carrier Hornet in this daring attempt to carry the war to the Japanese homeland. All of the planes dropped their bombs, but the flight ran into foul weather and most of the airmen either crash-landed or bailed out. Of eighty fliers, seventy-one survived. The damage to Tokyo was not significant, but this offensive strike was a strong boost to the morale of the American people.

In addition to supporting the Doolittle Raiders, the continuing storage of fuel at two bases north of Kunming was used to extend the range and increase the load capabilities of the American B-29s flying from the Mariana Islands to bomb Singapore and other Japanese-held areas. It was an effort of staggering proportions, its size matched only by the hazards involved. As Joe came to see the immensity and the danger of the job to be done, he couldn't help but wonder if he'd ever see his home and family again.

Here were the highest mountain peaks in the world combined with primitive navigational aids and notoriously bad weather. So numerous were the planes being lost trying to cross this forbidding mountain range, it was said you could find your way from India to China by following the trail of bits and pieces of aluminum airplane parts.

Pilots arriving from the states desperately needed to learn how to cope with the specialized weather and altitude problems they would meet here. So at Gaya, the Army set up the Transition School for Hump Pilots.

Constantly turbulent weather was a fact of life in this part of the world. The hot air from Burma thrust northward at speeds up to 150 MPH, where it collided violently with the cold Siberian air, resulting in strong thunderstorms and severe icing conditions.

Not only was the weather treacherous, but the terrain was inherently dangerous. The magnificent slopes and valleys, so awesome to view, were the very cause of extreme and unpredictable updrafts and downdrafts.

The risk to aircraft was compounded by the lack of up-to-date navigational aids that were taken for granted in more heavily-traveled parts of the world. There were few beacons en route between stations, and although non-directional radio beacons were available at some airports, they were of limited power.

When Joe arrived in Gaya, the commanding officer of the base was the school's Director of Operations. A fine officer, he had been a Link Trainer instructor for a U.S. airline, but he had little experience in bad weather flying.

He instructed Joe to write up a complete curriculum for a flight training school. Joe went out and flew the various routes from the bases in the Assam Valley into China and came back with information about the survival skills needed.

At the new school they taught the pilots meteorology, fine-tuned to the local weather conditions. They also briefed them on the importance of using oxygen at the extremely high altitudes they would be flying, and the proper way to use it.

One of the specific navigational problems the school taught these mostly unseasoned pilots was how to use the Automatic Direction Finder manually to locate non-directional beacons. Few of these pilots knew all that could be accomplished by utilizing the manual position on the ADF switch.

Months before, on that first B-17 trip from Romulus, Michigan to Prestwick, Scotland, ice had destroyed the sense antenna of those ADFs. In the same way, as these planes flew in and out of downdrafts, ice crystals would collect and build up on any solid surface of the plane that encountered that super-cooled moist air. The weight and rigidity of the ice would soon destroy the automatic functioning of the ADF, a necessary piece of equipment. The pilots were taught how to rotate the loop by hand and locate the heading to the station desired.

Much of what was done in the school at Gaya was patterned after TWA's school in Albuquerque, adapted to the local conditions. This kind of detail training was the critically important specialty of the Gaya school.

By March, 1944, all was well set up and every new pilot who came to fly the Hump had to be checked out in either a C-46 or a B-24 at the Gaya school.

The B-24s had turbo superchargers and were capable of the high-altitude flying necessary to clear the 20,000-foot mountains on the northernmost route. The C-46s flew a little further south where the mountains were not so high. DC-3s were also flown on the lower route.

From Gaya, the graduates were assigned to the various Assam Valley bases from which the Hump flights originated.

Periodically, all had to undergo check rides in the various planes, and on one occasion, a newly-appointed base commander was to give Joe an instrument check in a DC-3. They climbed in and the CO pulled the hood over Joe's cockpit so he could make an instrument takeoff.

Joe could still see a little off to his left where the hood had not covered the windshield completely. He could tell he was not lined up straight with the runway, yet he was being told to go ahead. So, straightening his line of takeoff, Joe headed down the runway. Of course, by his repositioning, the CO knew Joe could see somewhat, so he spent most of the remainder of the short flight reaching back and pushing the hood into place.

A lot of one-upmanship takes place in the military. Maybe the CO was looking forward to being able to correct Joe on his takeoff. After that initial sparring, however, the two men got along fine and worked together for many months.

Bombs, ammunition, trucks—all kinds of materials were flown across the Hump, but the primary and most essential cargo was aircraft fuel. In December, 1943, the month before Joe arrived, 6,000 tons were delivered and there was a steady push to increase the figures.

The vehicles for delivery of this important fuel to the Kunming area were both the B-24 and its cargo version, the C-87. There was an important difference, however, between these two planes. In the B-24, the fuel was carried in tanks that had been built to fit in the four bomb bays, but in the C-87, the bomb bay had been eliminated and the fuel was carried in 55-gallon steel drums loaded into the cabin.

These poorly-made drums, from local sources, were filled and sealed at sea level. When they were taken aloft to 25,000 feet or higher, they were subject to the stress of radical pressure changes. There might be a difference of as much as eight pounds between the air pressure within the drum and the thin air in the plane.

As the planes gained altitude coming up out of the Assam Valley to cross the Hump, often the crews would hear the sound of drum heads buckling under the expanding pressure from within. Then, sometimes they'd smell gas fumes from a leaking drum. Other times, the crew members weren't lucky enough to smell it.

Joe quickly realized one precaution they could take was to turn off the electric hydraulic pump. This pump was located in the cargo compartment very close to those drums of fuel. The arcing of the brushes in the electric motor could instantly ignite escaping fumes. Another source of ignition could be from the arcing of the contact points in the radio transmitters mounted on top of the center section of the wing. These are some examples of the safety tips passed on to the pilots in the school before they went out to confront these dangers.

In spite of the best of efforts, many planes exploded in flight because of the leaking gas drums. Carrying flammable cargo is always a danger, of course, and this deadly situation reveals clearly the expendability of life in wartime. Getting the fuel delivered was the name of the game, and if some planes didn't make it, that was the cost of the effort.

Flying heavily-loaded aircraft in mountainous terrain has its own hazards even without flammable cargo. A pilot is always at his busiest on takeoff. He is watching his airspeed, his heading, and especially his altimeter, looking for that critical increase in altitude which will show him he is off the ground. At this time, it is the co-pilot's responsibility to raise the retractable landing gear. This reduces the drag of the plane and assists the pilot's effort to climb quickly to a safe altitude.

On both versions of the B-24, the wheels retracted outward and upward into the wings of the plane. Because it was a high-wing plane, there was a considerable length to the gear strut, and the rising strut formed a large arc before it was safely tucked into the wing. It was thought that the gyroscopic action of the heavy spinning wheels, as they left the runway and began their movement upward, slowed the gear retraction. This was later found to be a negligible factor, but at this time, the co-pilot was ordered to apply the brakes as quickly as possible after the wheels left the runway, in order to stop the spinning action. Then, he was to lift the gear.

On at least one occasion, a plane was taking off and the co-pilot, thinking they were airborne, applied the brakes before the plane left the runway. The premature braking action slowed the takeoff run and the plane never got off the ground. It overran the end of the runway and all aboard were killed.

In early 1944, soon after Joe's arrival in the area, Allied planes had been diverted from the Chinese supply line and pressed into service hauling troops to Myitkyina, Burma, where the Japanese made a last-ditch effort. The year before they had captured Singapore from the British and they had fought their way up from the Malayan peninsula.

Joe had a one-night layover there at Myitkyina at that time, and learned a little about the contrast between this battle and the supply battle he had been fighting. At dusk, his tentmates calmly told him that he should not sleep on his cot, but on the ground underneath it.

"On more than one occasion," they told him, "Jap snipers infiltrated the compound and men were stabbed in their beds."

Where Joe had been working, the enemies were weather and poor equipment, and he was familiar with danger. But this kind of vulnerability was more personal than he cared for.

In a fierce battle there at Myitkyina, Lt. General Joseph Stilwell's troops were finally successful and the Japanese were turned back. In the latter months of the war, the greatly increased tonnage of the airlift into China was gradually supplemented even more by the trucks getting through on the Burma Road.

By August, 1944, the tonnage over the Hump had been raised to 20,000 tons in a month, the school was functioning well, and, with their thousandth student graduated, the men held a small celebration. The press relations officer took a picture of this special student, together

"SCHOOL FOR "HUMP" HOPPERS GRADUATES 1000th PILOT" was the header the Lafayette Leader ran over this photo, identical to the "classified" one Joe sent his wife in June, 1945. Left to right, Lt. Stanley J. Ralph, instructor; Maj. Joseph L. Halsmer, Director of Operations of the Gaya Transition School; Lt. Melvin O. Owens, 1000th graduate; and Maj. Jack A. Beaver, Los Angeles, the base Executive Officer.

with his training pilot, the executive officer, and Joe, standing by the prop of a B-24.

Joe sent his wife a copy of the picture but, due to censorship, he couldn't explain who the people were or what the occasion was. The military tightly restricted the passing of information about the names of units and places.

A few days after Josephine received the letter, the same picture, furnished by the Air Force with all the pertinent information, was printed in the Lafayette newspaper. Such are the ways of war.

Joe continued to fly the Hump regularly in order to keep abreast of the conditions under which the men were working. On one trip into China in the C-87, he encountered severe weather conditions and his ADF sense antenna was destroyed by ice. It was the blackest of nights, but making his approach by using the loop in the manual position, he let down through the overcast.

Just as he broke out of the cloud, about two miles out from the runway, he saw the huge exhaust flame of a B-24 coming directly at him. Quickly he dumped his plane downward and the oncoming plane passed closely overhead.

Joe felt like he could have reached up and touched it.

Miraculously, they'd had enough altitude to take that sudden dive and avoid striking the ground. Joe called the tower and complained about conflicting use of the runway, but to them, it was only another near miss.

By two o'clock in the morning, they were ready to pull out and return to the base in India. Freezing rain had begun to fall. Then Joe discovered there was a bad magneto on the plane, lessening the safety factor. So he turned it over to the maintenance department and he and his crew sacked out for a good night's sleep.

It's no wonder when the men returned to base after this kind of flying, that they would line up at the doctor's little office for their expected shot of booze. They needed something to help them relax and sleep that night and be ready for more of the same the next day.

Joe took his nip when he had been out on the line, but he looked forward with even greater anticipation to Sunday mornings when the Red Cross truck would come around after Mass. He really appreciated those chocolate-covered doughnuts they served with the coffee. Sunday morning family breakfasts had always featured special treats, so they were a sweet reminder of home.

Sundays were also special for Joe at Gaya because of the local Jesuit missionary, Father Jim Creane. There was no chaplain at the base, so Father Creane celebrated Mass for the men.

Joe went often to his poor little chapel in the village. There were so many holes in the thatched roof, a navigator could have taken star shots from inside. But he was a joyful, holy man who never complained, and Joe enjoyed spending time with him.

One of Joe's best friends at Gaya was his C-46 chief pilot. His name was Stew Lindke and he was a fine pilot and a good man. He often attended Mass with Joe even though he was not a Catholic. (His wife was. Maybe it made him feel closer to her when he went to church with Joe.)

Stew was a motorcycle enthusiast, and one day he and a couple of others asked Joe to help them with a project they had dreamed up to have a little fun.

A few miles away, at Asansol, was a salvage depot operated by the British. Stew had heard there were motorcycles in storage there that had been used in the Battle at Imphal.

If they could get a truck, they would go over and try to get some cycles for the pilots to enjoy when they were off duty. So Joe managed to get permission for them to use a four-by-four truck and a trailer. The following day they returned with six motorcycles in various stages of disassembly and a supply of extra parts.

It certainly raised the morale around the base for a long time while the men worked on those bikes. They finally got four of them running and they worked off a lot of steam racing them. There was always a need for ways to help the men forget their loneliness and the dangerous flying.

One night, two of the men decided to go tiger hunting. They drove a truck about thirty-five miles into the country, taking along a couple of Army rifles, a small goat they had purchased from one of the natives, and some wood with which to build a platform in a tree. They also had some aircraft landing lights with a battery for power.

When they found a clearing they thought a likely place, they tied up their little goat as bait. They set up the lights, ready to shine on the goat when the tiger appeared. They built a rough platform about twenty-five feet above the ground in a tree, and brought their battery wire to the platform so they could switch on the lights when they chose. Then they climbed onto their platform and settled down to wait in the growing dusk.

As the darkness deepened, the unfamiliar noises of the forest became more threatening. They remembered every story they had ever heard about vicious snakes, especially those that live in trees. They wondered what in the world they were doing in the snakes' own territory when the best defense against snakes is to avoid them. As time dragged on, there came to be, in fact, considerably more concern about their own defense than about any offense against a tiger.

A long period of stillness was interrupted by soft footfalls in the brush below. An unidentified sniffing brought forth a plaintive bleat from the goat, but while they were still deciding whether or not to flash on their lights, quiet reigned again.

The physical discomfort of their half-sitting, half-kneeling positions on the rough wood began to make minutes seem like hours. Added to this was the mental stress of having to keep their guns more or less at the ready for any development.

The tension of waiting in the dark was becoming unbearable. Then the men heard low growling and heavy breathing indicating the presence of some large animal. A tiger?

As told later, when they had returned to the base with empty hands, each accused the other of having whispered: "Let's be real quiet. Maybe he'll go away!"

The men were better pilots than hunters.

There were good men at Gaya and they persevered. In July, 1945, the last full month of war, a total of 69,000 tons of cargo was carried over the Hump. But it was expensive freight hauling. In forty months, it cost 250 planes and the lives of 850 men.

Busy as he was with the supply effort, Joe was not exempt from the military's well-known red tape or "paper blizzard." Manpower was at such a premium that flying officers were required to do things ordinarily done by the administrative staff. Joe served on the Board of Accident Investigation, which kept him busy, and on the Flying Evaluation Board. There was also a Court Martial Board that met occasionally.

In October, 1944, Joe was overdue for a promotion to the rank of major. His commanding officer told him that his recommendation for the promotion had been "returned... in conformity with ICD-ATC Reg. 35-14...."

A second promotion request had been "received in this Headquarters on December 17, 1944, too late for consideration during the month of December."

Only after all his papers were in his possession at the war's end did Joe learn more about the cause of the delay.

When the CO had resubmitted his request and asked the reason for the delay, he got an angry response. The regular Army brass were disgusted with field officers who had little knowledge and even less respect for the intricacies of Army rules and regulations.

To quote briefly: "This Headquarters has no intention of requesting information from the India Wing Commander as to why it took twelve days for the recommendation for subject officer to arrive... after initiation by your Headquarters.... It is further pointed out the Wing Commander is not responsible for reporting his actions to your Headquarters.... Had your unit been fully familiar with current regulations.... Your attitude... will not facilitate or expedite.... Your attention is directed to the fact that recommendations arriving in this Headquarters after the twelfth of the month will not normally be considered until the following month."

In early 1945, Joe finally did receive his promotion to the rank of major, and was appointed Director of Operations of the school he had been managing for over a year.

Whenever he had a little time to himself, Joe still pondered the right design for a combination machine that could be flown for long distances and then driven on city streets for convenience. He wanted to be able to fold the wings in such a way that they could be kept with the vehicle. He considered it impractical and inconvenient to have to leave the wings somewhere and return later to retrieve them.

Another problem to be overcome was how to protect people from the propeller when the vehicle was on the ground. If he used a pusher prop at the rear, it could be protected by the folded wings. Many ideas simmered in his mind, but they would have to wait until he had the time and place to build them into a working model.

Time spent overseas was supposed to be limited to one and a half or two years. This was Joe's second summer in India and he hoped that, before long, he would be going home.

The war was beginning to turn around. The Allies had landed troops on the continent in Europe and were on the offensive in the Pacific. The defeat of the Japanese at Myitkyina had been a critical turning point. That was their last threat to the Burma Road and the Chinese supply line.

Joe's commanding officer took another chance with the brass at headquarters and recommended him to receive the Bronze Star Medal. He cited Joe's work in "the establishment of procedures for high-altitude flying under the most adverse conditions over the India-China air routes, and for the difficult letdowns necessary in China ...." He wrote that Joe had "pioneered the development of standard flying maneuvers for use in the China, Burma, and India Theaters... displayed remarkable judgment and common sense.... His leadership inspired a high degree of devotion to duty among students and pilot instructors and played a vital role in the success of the transition school of the India China Division, Air Transport Command."

Joe was honored to receive such an award, but the paper from headquarters he liked best was the one he received in late July, 1945. It relieved him of his duties in the CBI Wing of the Air Transport Command, and transferred him to Romulus AFB in Romulus, Michigan with thirty days leave at home en route.

Joe flew to Karachi and took the military shuttle plane, a C-87, to the southern coast of the Arabian peninsula; across Africa to Accra; to Ascension Island; to Natal, Brazil; to Caracas, Venezuela; to Dutch Guiana; then to Miami, and finally home.

India was a hot and dirty place, and Joe shed no tears when he left. He arrived home on August 15, 1945, V-J Day.

Josephine's mother was with her and the two little boys, so the happy reunited couple went downtown to have dinner together. The whole nation was riotously celebrating Japan's acceptance of the surrender terms. The streets were full of people yelling, dancing, blowing horns, and venting the tensions of the long war years in all kinds of crazy behavior. They couldn't find a single restaurant where anyone was interested in serving meals. Finally, in frustration, they returned home and had their own celebration with leftovers from the refrigerator.

After his thirty-day leave, the family spent eight weeks at Romulus before Joe received his separation papers. Where three and a half years earlier the Air Force was recruiting men into its ranks as quickly as it could absorb them, now authorities were anxious to reverse the tide. By early November, the Halsmers were "back home again in Indiana."

HEADQUARTERS
INDIA CHINA DIVISION
AIR TRANSPORT COMMAND
1300th AAF Base Unit

GENERAL ORDERS)
           :
NUMBER   47)

                                            APO 192 % Postmaster
                                            New York City, N. Y.
                                            28 July 1945

E X T R A C T

*   *   *   *   *   *

II.   AWARDS OF THE BRONZE STAR MEDAL

        1. Pursuant to the authority contained in Army Regulations 600-45 (C 3), War Department, Washington, D. C., dated 22 September 1943, as amended, the Bronze Star Medal is hereby awarded to the following named officers and enlisted man:

*   *   *   *   *   *

JOSEPH L. HALSMER, 0480897, Major, Air Corps, for distinguishing himself by meritorious service in connection with military operations against the enemy during the period 11 March 1944 to 6 April 1945. Home address: 232 Marstellar Street, West Lafayette, Indiana.

*   *   *   *

                              /s/ William H Tunner
                              /t/ WILLIAM H TUNNER
                      Brigadier General, U. S. Army
                                 Commanding

DISTRIBUTION "S"

A TRUE EXTRACT COPY:

J. B. GROSSMAN
Major, Air Corps

Award of the Bronze Star Medal to Major Joseph L. Halsmer, U.S. Army Air Corps, by Brigadier General William H. Tunner, USA Commanding, 28 July, 1945.

Josephine and Joe before the Cub Cruiser as new partnership of Halsmer Flying Service assumes operation of Halsmer airport, 1945.

CHAPTER 6

BACK IN INDIANA — OCCASIONALLY

The beginnings of the international air cargo business

Throughout the whole country there was a great sense of relief that the war was over. Everyone expected to return joyfully to jobs and homes. However no homes had been constructed during the war, so there were few places available either to rent or to buy. For many people it would be a long road back to normal life.

Joe moved his wife and family into the now empty farmhouse where he had grown up. Although this house had long ago been electrified, it had never had water piped indoors. So on those late fall evenings, after the two little boys were in bed, Joe and Josephine worked together, installing pipes and building a bathroom. In the daytime, with his brothers, Joe plunged into rebuilding their business. They took over operation of the airport from the friend who had leased it during the war and formed Halsmer Flying Service. Included in the new partnership was good friend Ray Korty, one of their earliest flying companions.

The first order of business for the young company was to acquire some rolling stock and, thereby, some income. So the partners became Aeronca dealers and bought a two-place trainer. They also bought a Cub Cruiser, a J-3 Cub, and, a little later, a four-place Aeronca Sedan. This latter turned out to be an excellent plane both for charter work and banner towing.

An early major step forward for the men was the purchase of the 100

Halsmer homestead in 1945 when Joe and Josephine moved in.

acres of land that lay adjacent to the south. The brothers did not like the idea of incurring indebtedness and at first were reluctant. But the realtor advised them, quite insistently, to take advantage of this opportunity to expand, so they borrowed enough to make the purchase. There was a large barn on the property and they remodeled it into an office building. The added land enabled them to improve the position of their runway.

The airport business was a seven-day-a-week job, and evenings and weekends were the busiest times. At first all three brothers worked every day and every weekend, but eventually, each took one weekday off. They all liked it better than the dairy business and were glad to have people interested in flying.

In the spring of 1946, Joe got a phone call from his old friend and former chief C-46 pilot in India, Stew Lindke. Stew wanted Joe to go with him to Ponca City, Oklahoma to pick up a B-17 and help him to fly it to his hometown of Croswell, Michigan. The American Legion Post there wanted to set it up as a memorial.

Joe agreed and he and Stew took an airline flight to Oklahoma to check the records of the planes available. Hundreds of war surplus planes had been put in dead storage at Ponca City by the armed forces. Most were being systematically destroyed since there was no market for them. To a pilot like Joe, it was heartbreaking to see a large hoist drop a thick blade of steel on a wing, chopping it off the fuselage in a single blow; to watch a Caterpillar grind its way across the wreckage, crushing it, then pushing the mutilated fuselage into a large open-end furnace where the whole thing was turned into a mass of molten aluminum.

But they turned to the business at hand and after inspecting several planes, they decided on one they thought might be the best buy. The machine they chose had corroded cylinders, a result of long idleness, but they got it started. On the way north, the engine ran dry of oil west of Chanute Field in central Illinois. By declaring an emergency situation on their radio, they were allowed to land on the military field. There they refilled all four engines with oil and completed the flight to Michigan uneventfully.

At Croswell, the only available landing place was a 2,500-foot grass field with a wooded area on the far end. Anticipating the need for the shortest possible landing roll, Joe began braking as they came in over the fence. He held the nose high and put the tailwheel down first. They got stopped in 2,000 feet with maximum brake and the trees were staring them in the face.

That visit to Ponca City alerted Joe and his brothers to the opportunities available there in war surplus airplanes. With only a little modification, the FAA would certify the AT-6s and the BT-13s for use in advanced instructing and air show work.

Joe flew down there again with Johnny and after thorough examination, they bought an AT-6 and five BT-13s and made arrangements to get them home.

That July, Halsmer Flying Service produced its first air show. The young company wanted to publicize all the ways in which it could be of service to the community. It offered flight instruction, charter service, ambulance service, aerial advertising, maintenance, hangar rental, and gas and oil sales.

The men planned the various attractions, promoted, and sold tickets. On the big day, Johnny and Joe demonstrated the maneuverability and speed of the BT-13s and the AT-6. They used the Aeronca Champs for a ribbon-cutting contest, and got five friends to put on a ten lap race with the BT-13s.

The Air Force had been invited to send their P-80 over from Dayton, Ohio. People always enjoyed this demonstration of speed up to 500 MPH.

A couple of parachute jumps climaxed the show, and according to the next issue of the Lafayette Journal Courier, it "thrilled 10,000 spectators, only half of whom were able to get into the field to pay an attendance charge of seventy-five cents." The rest "watched the show from automobiles parked on surrounding roads."

The young businessmen did well on the air show, but Halsmer Flying

Stewart Lindke and Halsmer after landing the B-17 in the small field at Croswell, Mich., 1946.

Service was not exactly setting the world on fire as a money-making proposition. In the fall, Joe and Josephine were expecting their third child. Johnny now had a wife and baby to support, and Hank was planning his wedding. There were a few students and a budding charter business, but the families were growing faster than the business.

So it was with great excitement and anticipation that Joe received a phone call one day from an old friend of his Romulus days. Henry Renninger was in New York with Ray and Art Norden and other Air Force friends who wanted to start a cargo airline. The men planned to specialize in hauling cargo by air, concentrating on pickups along the east coast and flying to the west coast. The name they had chosen was Seaboard and Western Airlines. Would Joe be interested in helping?

It didn't take Joe long to tell Henry he would be right over to help them get off the ground, literally. Johnny and Hank were also offered the opportunity to join this new venture, but they preferred to stay with the Indiana business. So it was decided: Joe would fly for Seaboard, retaining his interest in Halsmer Flying Service. Both the brothers at home would fly charter and instruct students, but Johnny would run the maintenance shop and Hank would administer the business affairs.

Halsmer Flying Service AT-6, acquired at Ponca City, Okla., 1946.

Shortly after this decision, the fourth partner and friend, Ray Korty, joined Seaboard for a short time before moving on to Flying Tiger Airlines. Until his death in 1973, Ray flew all over the world for Tigers while retaining his partnership in Halsmer Flying Service.

The new company quickly acquired its first DC-4 and got it modified for commercial use. This four-motored transport was the workhorse of the military during the war, widely used both for troops and supplies. It carried 18,000 pounds of payload at a cruising speed of 180 miles per hour and was a joy to fly. It could carry as much as 3,200 gallons of fuel and could stay in the air seventeen hours.

The first shipping orders Seaboard received were for cargo delivery to Europe. Trans-Atlantic, middle eastern, and even far eastern business grew rapidly. So from the beginning, Seaboard was an international carrier. Nine years later the company changed its name to Seaboard World Airlines, Inc.

In the DC-4, the trip from New York to Gander, Newfoundland was a five-and-a-half-hour flight. It took another nine hours to get to Shannon, Ireland, and three more hours to Amsterdam, Holland. On return trips, they always had to fight headwinds, so they could count on a twelve- or thirteen-hour water leg westbound.

In spite of the well-earned, notorious reputation of the North Atlantic weather, Joe was happy to be flying through it.

"How lucky I am," he thought.

Before the war, the prospects for his future looked like a choice between the dull stability of milking cows or the gypsy-like life of a barnstormer. Now, here he was, in the exciting position of being the pilot of one of about 12 planes out over the Atlantic at any one time, with a respected and well-paid professional career.

One night on one of those early eastbound flights, Joe came upon a long weather front lying directly across his plane's path. He had been seeing lightning flash both to the right and left up ahead for some time. It was an extremely large storm and with no way to get around it or above it, there was nothing to do but plow ahead. As the rough air gave them tooth-jarring bounce after bounce, there was a sense of being wholly at the mercy of the storm. Joe remembered how scared he was as a five-year-old when Pop sent him one night out to the milk house to bring him his hammer. Just as he had those many years ago, he pressed his lips together and did what he had to do.

Then, with a horrendous crash, the DC-4 took a lightning strike directly on the nose.

Stunned, unable to see a thing, and still blinded with no knowledge of what damage the plane might have sustained, Joe was clearly aware, in those next moments, of the distinctly reassuring sound of the humming of the engines.

His first thought was, "Well, whatever has happened, at least the engines are still running!"

As they continued on, no further problelms developed, their eyesight returned to normal, and they decided they were okay. Later, on the ground, when they examined the plane, they found several pinpoint holes the lightning had burned in the metal deck in front of the windshield. That and the momentary blindness of the crew was fortunately the only damage.

On those early flights into Germany, the devastation of the cities was a shock to see. Where the Allies had bombed so thoroughly only two years earlier, now the people were out in the streets resolutely pulling apart the rubble with their bare hands, using what bricks they could find for new structures.

Some of the first flights went into Luxembourg, a pretty little country, where there was little war damage. Others went to Schiphol Airport in Amsterdam; or to London. Every flight had a story all its own. A typical load might have taken wearing apparel, pharmaceuticals, textiles, animals, or machines to London, England; Paris, France; Geneva, Switzerland; or Frankfurt or Munich, Germany. Soon there were also contracts with the military to fly either supplies or personnel.

At that time Seaboard was flying out of MacArthur Field on Long Island, and one night Joe left there to pick up a load at Dover Air Force Base in Massachusetts. Upon arrival at Dover, he onloaded 20,000 pounds of cholera serum destined for Egypt.

This was a maximum payload for the DC-4, necessitating shorter flight legs to refuel more often, so they went through Goose Bay, Labrador, and headed for Iceland.

About an hour into the flight, there was an explosion in the belly of the forward section of the plane. Immediately, they discovered they had no hydraulic pressure. This was no problem in flight, but in order to land, hydraulic pressure would be needed to activate the gear and flaps.

As they continued on, Joe and his engineer decided on a plan for repair of the system.

There was an opening in the floor behind the cockpit which leads into the belly of the plane, familiarly called the "hell hole." Leaving the flying to the co-pilot, the two men crawled down there and discovered that the hydraulic reservoir had blown up, and the system had lost all its fluid.

Elliott Held, the engineer, was an excellent mechanic, and together he and Joe found the lines to the hydraulic pump. Using the broken tubing, they replumbed a handmade system. Normal flight supplies always included three or four extra one-gallon cans of hydraulic fluid. Using one of those cans as a reservoir, they refilled the system. Now, when it became necessary, they would be able to pump the gear and flaps down manually.

As they proceeded, the weather became worse. They arrived over Keflavik, Iceland, at four in the morning to find the winds at eighty knots and the ceiling at 100 feet. The field was closed because the storm had knocked out all electricity to the control tower. That included the elimination of the Ground Controlled Approach system.

The GCA is a radar system that scans the runway approach area horizontally and vertically. It provides the pilot with his position and elevation on the final approach pattern.

About fourteen miles away was a field at Reykjavik, but its runway was inadequate for this large heavily-loaded plane. However, Reykjavik did have a range station, one leg of which crossed over the Keflavik field.

Joe decided he could get into the closed Keflavik field using that range leg in spite of the fact that its radio signals fourteen miles out would be weak and wide.

He had little choice. Joe took the plane over the range station and proceeded out the NW leg, listening to the dot-dash and the dash-dot on either side of the range leg.

It was difficult to stay on that range leg with the winds gusting so, but when he was on center, he heard the merged signal. If he could stay on the leg for fourteen miles and descend through the dense fog to 100 feet, he hoped to be able to see the runway lights on the field below.

Plowing through the heavy fog, being buffeted by the strong winds was too much for the co-pilot. About the time Joe's calculations told him they should be over Keflavik, the co-pilot became disoriented.

Suffering from vertigo, he began screaming at the top of his voice, "We're going to crash! We're going to crash!"

Joe had to ignore him as he began his letdown.

When they were down to 100 feet, Joe caught a glimpse of the runway lights at ninety degrees to his course. Holding his heading for thirteen seconds, he then started a 270 degree turn to the left—all this while the ship was bouncing around in the eighty-knot wind and the co-pilot still screaming in terror.

He tried to hold a three-degree-per-second rate for the 270 degree turn. As he finished turning and began further descent, there, directly in front of them, was the runway. A general sense of relief swept over the cockpit as one spoke for all.

"Best looking runway I ever saw!"

The co-pilot was all apologies. His breakdown was unintentional, of course, but it proves that complete trust in one's instruments is absolutely necessary.

The makeshift hydraulic system had gotten them down, but since they had no steering or brakes, a tug had to pull them to the hangar. The plane required three days of maintenance there before they could proceed.

At Amsterdam, another ton of cholera serum was added to the load and they took off for Cairo. The Egyptian Minister of Health and several other dignitaries met the plane at the airport to express personally their thanks for the cholera serum. That was pleasant, but the primary feelings of the crew were relief to be finished with another demanding trip.

Joe's main interest when he had delivered a load anywhere in the world was to get what rest he needed and then point his plane for home. As time went by, the commuting to New York became more of a nuisance. Joe loved being back in the big ships he had flown during the war, but he hated being away from his family for days at a time. Perhaps after this third baby arrived, he and Josephine would move to

New York.

At that time, each trip was requiring from six to fifteen days. Probably half of that was layover time between the legs of a trip. FAA regulations limited the number of hours a pilot could fly without rest. When a DC-4 crew had flown a twelve- or thirteen-hour flight leg, they would have to disembark and a rested crew waiting at that stop would go on with the plane. Most crew members (except for a few free-spirited bachelors) were always hoping to cut down on that time away from home. Joe's own travel time was increased, of course, by that additional spur between New York and Indiana.

So, after some househunting on Long Island, Joe signed a lease on a furnished half of a big, rambling old double at 279 Handsome Avenue, in Sayville, a pleasant little village on the south shore of Long Island. He hoped Josephine would like it.

On the 24th of September, their first daughter, Marianna, was born. Six weeks later, they packed the three children and all their personal belongings into the blue, torpedo-body Pontiac and drove to New York.

That fall, enroute home from Shannon, Joe had a trip with a light freight load, with fifty-knot headwinds predicted. They would fly west to Gander with enough fuel to divert to Stephenville if necessary, plus fuel for two hours of holding time. The crew expected a normal trip.

After the end of the war, the Coast Guard had stationed ships out in the north Atlantic for the purpose of relaying up-to-date weather information to the ever-growing number of planes crossing and recrossing the ocean.

Fighting those headwinds that morning, soon after passing Coast Guard Ocean Station Charlie, there was one fantastic roar as the number two engine ran wild. The prop had snapped into fine pitch and was uncontrollable.

They were flying at cruise power when it happened, and the prop went from 1,800 RPM to over 3,000 RPM. In this situation, there was a real danger that the tremendous force of the windmilling prop could throw a blade and possibly pierce the fuselage.

Joe immediately pulled back the throttle, hit the feathering button, and cut off the fuel mixture. But all control to the prop was lost and it still continued to windmill at 2,800 RPM. He reduced the airspeed of the plane to 130 knots, and that did slow the prop to 2,500 RPM. But those headwinds were a distinct problem. Pitting his 130-knot airspeed against the fifty-knot headwind was giving him a true speed of only eighty knots.

They were beyond the point of returning to Ireland, so they had two choices. They could ditch the plane at Ocean Station Charlie or they could continue their effort to reach Gander.

Joe and his navigator, receiving weather information from Charlie as well as from Gander and Shannon, carefully weighed every factor in this precarious situation.

They were presently flying in ice crystals and snow, and that was not expected to improve. The plane's reduced airspeed altered its attitude in the air, significantly lowering the tail. This changed position not only reduced the streamlining advantage, it also contributed to the buildup of ice on the leading edge and lower side of the wing. The worried crew knew their fuel supply was marginal. The additional hindrance of the ice was simply another negative factor to be considered.

Weighing the pros and cons of a deliberate ditching in the rough open sea, Joe made the decision to continue toward Gander.

There were a few more positive actions he could take. He brought the plane down to about 300 feet above the ocean's surface, hoping that the salt spray might de-ice the underside. A small rise in air temperature and slightly lessened head winds at the lower altitude were of some benefit.

In an effort to conserve all the fuel possible, he shut off the cabin heat. Joe knew that the extreme cold could endanger the shipment of live canaries they had aboard, but he was balancing this against the possible loss of the plane and the crew, as well as the cargo, in the sea.

By this time, the Air Sea Rescue Service had been alerted. This rescue station, attached to the U.S. Air Force Base at Stephenville, Newfoundland, dispatched a B-17 to find the crippled plane. They would be prepared to drop the rescue boat they carried to help the crew survive if they had to ditch.

The determined Seaboard men pressed on toward Gander.

The first direct radio contact the DC-4 had from the rescue plane informed them that he had inadvertently passed them and was approximately fifty miles to the east. He suggested that the struggling cargo plane turn and fly eastward toward him to make visual contact with each other.

"Ring again, brother," was Joe's response. "You've got the wrong number!"

He wasn't about to turn away from his Gander heading with his limited fuel supply and head back out toward the open ocean!

"He has plenty of gas. Let him find me," muttered Joe to himself.

Still about fifty miles out, they limped toward the coastline. Now they could see the jagged top of the pack ice, jammed by the wind against the Newfoundland coast. Coming down in that would shred the plane like cabbage cut for slaw.

By this time, the fuel gauges were registering empty. It was the only time the crew found the inaccuracy of their instruments something to joke about.

As they passed over the iceberg field and came in sight of the coast, occasional frozen lakes were visible among the trees.

"I could put down on one of those lakes if I had to. Heck of a lot better than out in open water... or on that pack ice!" Joe breathed a little more easily.

As they neared the Gander strip, he reduced his altitude so that he could take advantage of emergency procedure. Straight in on the runway they landed, with no approach delay. When attendants stuck the tanks with their long dipsticks, there was no measurable fuel left.

Mechanics pulled the plane into the hangar and took the dome off the prop. There they found a threaded steel plug that had fallen off the end of the crankshaft. Evidently it had not been secured in positon. The loss of this plug from the end of the crankshaft caused the oil pressure to fail, and oil pressure controls the propeller. In about three hours, the plane was refueled, repaired, and ready to go on to New York.

The canaries survived.

But that was not to be the end of this trip. As the flight neared New York, the weary crew learned an enormous snowstorm was in progress along the east coast, and New York was closed in tight. They were diverted to Washington, D.C., and had to wait there for two days before they could return to New York.

This saga began on Christmas Eve with Joe's family expecting his arrival that evening for all the usual family fun. In addition, at the Halsmer home were four house guests from Indiana who had come for the Christmas holidays. There had been elaborate plans for their visit, but as it turned out, they all enjoyed the twenty-four inch snowfall and Christmas without Joe. He got home on December 27, two days before the friends were to return home.

With all the travel problems the snow caused, this was one time Joe was glad he had moved to New York.

In these early days, there was a tremendous esprit de corps among the Seaboard people. Everyone worked hard to enable the company to stay on its feet. It was the kind of spirit that helped all to wait patiently when paychecks could not be written on time, and it was in this spirit that the pilots avoided any unnecessary delays and kept the planes flying. They knew that a plane sitting on the ground was costing the company money.

Once on the ground in Iceland, as Joe gave his plane its usual walkaround inspection, he saw a hole in the exhaust manifold. It was in a position that enabled the exhaust gases to fire against the dishpan, which is a plate on the side of the fuselage placed there for protection from exhaust heat.

It was a hazardous situation to have burning gas released through this hole instead of out the tailpipe at the back. If the extreme heat were to burn through the dishpan, it could cause considerable damage to engine accessories in that section of the plane.

Joe went to the maintenance building, looked around a bit, and found a piece of a P-80 tailpipe. He borrowed some tools from one of the mechanics there, cut the metal to fit, and welded it onto the exhaust manifold to close the hole. It wasn't the only time Joe went the extra mile for Seaboard.

But there were some less admirable incidents too.

The long hours the crews spent in the cockpit required intense concentration as they continually monitored their instruments. Combine this sustained mental effort with physical inactivity and you get exhaustion. Some people relieve that kind of stress with practical jokes.

One time when there was a new first officer aboard, the radioman and Joe took advantage of his inexperience.

On the floor near the feet of the radioman was a small hole covered by a flap. Through it, emergency flares could be dropped if needed. The radioman could lift this flap with his toe, and when it was up about an inch, it caused a low roaring noise like a foghorn.

Also involved in this prank was a strap over the captain's head. Pulled down and fastened to a lever on the floor, its purpose was to lock the control surfaces on the wings.

As they were taking off from Amsterdam and heading out over the water, Joe gave the radioman a prearranged cue. When Joe pulled down on the overhead strap, the radioman gently lifted the flap over the hole, producing the foghorn sound.

They did this in accord a couple of times, and finally the new man simply had to ask, "What is that?"

"Why," Joe solemnly replied, "that's the foghorn we have to sound when we come out over the harbor to warn all those boats down there."

The new man kept his thoughts to himself, but shortly after, when he thought no one noticed, he reached up and pulled on the strap over the captain's head.

He was on the right track. The radioman didn't notice, so there was no responding sound.

But Joe noticed, so with a straight face he said sadly, "Well, now you did it. You broke the foghorn. I'll have to put that in the plane log."

And Joe reached for the aircraft logbook in which is entered all pertinent information about the flight and aircraft. And he wrote, "Foghorn broken," and duly noted the time and date.

It shook the new man up a little, but only briefly. He soon learned the details of the little joke.

On another occasion when there was a new co-pilot aboard a cargo flight, the crew played a prank on him in mid-ocean.

While the new man was at the controls, the others lifted the plate that covers the entry to the hell hole, and one by one, they let themselves down into the belly of the plane.

By raising the cover a trifle, Joe could see him in his seat. The new man soon noticed that everyone had left the cockpit and after several looks backward, he set the plane on automatic pilot and walked back into the cabin. He didn't see anyone, so he returned to the cockpit.

After more backward looks, he got up again, searched the whole cabin, and this time, he didn't sit down. He paced around the cockpit obviously worried.

"How did I manage to become the only person aboard this plane out here in the middle of the Atlantic?"

About that time, Joe got careless with his peeking, and the new man noticed the slightly-lifted floorplate.

Foolish tricks for grown men to play? Another crew had a different idea of fun.

This crew was bringing a load of military men and their families back to the US after their term of service in Germany, and they thought the servicemen would appreciate a good joke. So they gave the plane a few mild dips and waggles, and then the navigator opened the door between the cockpit and the cabin and rolled an empty liquor bottle down the cabin floor.

As the company grew, the crews encountered one another in the weather and operations offices all over Europe and the Middle East. Once, as Joe was getting ready to taxi out with a load of passengers at Brussels, Belgium, he heard another Seaboard pilot on the radio telling the tower to cancel his flight plan. He recognized the voice of his good friend, Ev Keeler, so he called him on VHF.

"What's the matter, Ev?"

"Oh, Joe, that you? I can't get my number three engine started. Starter locked up or something, I guess."

"Well, Ev, hang in there a few minutes. Don't offload your passengers yet. If you'll just taxi over to where there is more room on the ramp area, I'll give you some help."

As they moved into position, Joe explained his plan to park so that Ev could pull his plane up behind Joe, lining up his faulty engine directly behind Joe's number one engine.

"Get as close as you can, Ev, and let me know when you're ready. Partially feather your prop, and when I run up number one, I'm sure it will spin your prop and start your engine."

While Joe sat there waiting for Ev to maneuver into position, he thought how satisfying his life was.

"What a wonderful career flying has provided for me," Joe mused. "The world is shrinking as a result of mass air transportation. Maybe some day, as the people of the world get to know one another better, we can all become friends." It made him feel good to think he was a part of that.

Ev was behind him now and Joe began to rev his engine gently. When Joe's manifold pressure rose to thirty-five inches, Ev called out, "It's running, Joe, it's running!"

He took off right behind Joe and they agreed to do the same thing at Shannon, if necessary. But whatever was stuck in Ev's starter gave him no more trouble, and both made it back to New York without further problems.

In the fall of '47, one interesting flight led to the Halsmers' going into downtown New York to see Ethel Merman's hit Broadway play, "Annie Get Your Gun."

The New York cast of the play decided to take advantage of the publicity opportunity of the coming Thanksgiving holiday. Since Thanksgiving is not celebrated in England, they arranged to send two frozen turkeys to the British cast of the same play, for their holiday dinner, by way of Seaboard air freight. Their public relations man brought some members of the cast to the airport to present the turkeys to the crew for the flight, and pictures were duly taken by the newspeople. Joe happened to be the captain of this crew. When the picture-taking concluded, the PR man handed Joe a couple of tickets to the play and invited him to come backstage to meet Miss Merman after the show.

A few weeks later, the Halsmers took a subway train into Manhattan and enjoyed their first Broadway production. To see a show on Broadway was the fulfillment of one of Josephine's childhood dreams, so she was completely thrilled by the occasion. It wasn't until they were on the train en route back to Sayville that Joe remembered the backstage invitation. The failure to meet Miss Merman was a disappointment to Josephine. She couldn't imagine how anyone could overlook such a momentous opportunity, but that small misdeed only slightly dimmed her joy in a lovely evening on the town.

Living on Long Island wasn't all Joe had hoped it would be. He missed his association with his brothers in the airport business, and he missed the shop with all his tools and experimental projects. It was a long winter.

By the coming of the new year, the Halsmers began thinking seriously of moving back to Indiana. Perhaps commuting would be a better choice than living on the east coast after all.

Their Long Island lease would expire at the end of May, so in March, Josephine's mother came to stay with the children while Joe and Josephine went to Indiana to look for a place to live.

In Indiana, as well as nationwide, homes were still scarce and prices of homes and lots were rising at unbelievable rates.

After looking at everything available, they learned that the acreage across the road from the airport might be for sale. A beautiful wooded pasture, always attractive to the young couple, this property had been tied up in the settlement of an estate for years. Now, two days before they were to return east, Joe learned it might be available.

As they made frantic efforts to contact the people involved, they also did some serious praying.

Time was running out when they finally located Mr. S. and asked him to sell them ten acres of the woods for their home. At first he was reluctant, but he finally agreed to the sale.

Now they had land. They talked to a local manufacturer of prebuilt two- and three-bedroom homes. But, with a fourth child expected, they needed more room than that. National Homes didn't want to lose a sale, so they made some adjustment in their largest model and offered the Halsmers their first four-bedroom design. The happy couple arranged to have it set up on their lot, and prepared to return east the following day.

The next morning, a destructive windstorm swept through the community. They were shocked to learn of considerable damage at the airport. The hangar was untouched, but six planes that had been tied down outside were blown about and wrecked.

Hank had recently moved his family into a small apartment they'd had built in the office building. In the storm, Louise and their small daughter were shaken up when the roof was torn off the building, but they were unhurt.

After a quick look at the damage, Joe and Josephine had to leave the rebuilding to others and return east. But now they could look forward to the move back to Indiana and a new home.

CHAPTER 7

AT HOME ABROAD

*Berlin Airlift—A suicidal
race horse—6 frisky elephants*

At the end of May when their lease expired, the Halsmers loaded
their belongings into the old Pontiac and headed west, a move
that changed the course of their lives substantially. At the
same time, world leaders in Europe were making decisions that would
also greatly affect, not only the Halsmers' lives, but the lives of millions
of people in Europe and America.

At the war's end in 1945, the Allied forces from the western sector
had met the Russian troops in Berlin. This was the final collapse of the
German Reich and the victory the Allies had awaited with hope. But
the compromises of the restructured German government resulted in a
touchy political situation.

Three hundred thousand Russian troops surrounded Berlin at the
time of Germany's surrender and the Western Allies allowed Russia to
retain control of this occupied territory, including the contiguous land
east to the Russian border.

Germany was now divided, with the part under Russian control
renamed East Germany. Berlin was to be administered jointly by
English, French, Russian, and American forces, and the city itself was
split into East and West Berlin.

Because of past experiences, Berliners were much more fearful of
their Russian conquerors than of the Western Allies. Now they found
themselves isolated, an island of some two-and-a-half million people

behind the Russian lines. Devastated by the war, their food and supplies of all kinds were down to almost nothing.

The Allied nations were determined to help their former enemies rebuild and began supplying the city by trucks and train.

In the spring of 1948, however, the Russian government decided to extend the pressure of what was already being called the cold war. Its military forces began systematic harrassment of the supply route from the west. Their plan was to intimidate the Allies into abandoning Berlin into their hands. First, for insignificant reasons, they delayed trains and trucks carrying food and fuel, holding up needed supplies.

Then, what had begun as harrassment turned into an open show of Soviet power. They proclaimed a stop to all rail, road, and water traffic between Berlin and the west.

The Allies were resolute about continuing their support for the Germans, and the Berlin airlift came into being.

The American military command promptly contacted commercial air carriers for assistance and Seaboard was one of several awarded a contract to fly in supplies. Within ten days the total daily load into Berlin had reached 1,000 tons. Impressive as that was, Berlin would need four times that amount daily to survive. Along with the coal and food, the Allies began to include raw materials to keep factories open and people working. They were determined to show the Russians the depth of their commitment to the German community.

Often Joe made four trips a day into Berlin, shuttling back and forth from Frankfurt. As the operation became better organized and administered, manufactured goods were flown back out. There might be a load of radios, for instance, made in Berlin and bound for Turkey. In those cases, the cargo would be flown directly to its destination.

At first the Russians made no effort to hamper the supply train by air. They figured it was a small bandage applied to a bleeding wound. But when they saw the growing scope of the Allied effort, they determined to make the air assistance as difficult as possible. They made it clear that they would hold the western planes to a corridor of airspace only twenty miles wide and up to 10,000 feet high from West Germany into Berlin. They proclaimed that they would shoot down any planes straying outside that corridor. It became a life-threatening game of cat and mouse. Russian planes flew through Allied formations, trying to force the planes out of the corridor. American P-47's patrolled the space, confirming instrument readings and warning crews if they flew too close to the corridor boundaries where they could become subject to gunfire.

All the American planes used the same radio frequency and there was chatter back and forth. When a Russian Yak fighter hassled Joe once, someone on the radio quipped: "Throw a piece of coal at him!"

On Joe's first trip into Berlin, the ceiling at Templehof was right down on the ground and he couldn't see a thing. When Joe's altimeter showed he was only seventy-five feet above the ground, he was shaken by the sight of the walls of buildings on either side of him. Worse yet, below, he could see a cemetery.

"I sure hope that GCA man knows what he's doing," Joe fretted uneasily. "I'm in his hands."

Actually, the best air traffic control people in the world worked Templehof and Rhein-Main Airports in Berlin at that time and Joe knew it. In the next second, he saw before him the approach lights and runway. He landed, a little breathless but safe.

It took only fifteen minutes for the ground personnel to offload each flight. While they worked, the crew, who never left the plane, was handed hot coffee and doughnuts from a Red Cross truck that pulled up to the cockpit. That snack hit the spot, and as soon as the reloading was completed, they'd get out of there.

For many months this support went on, twenty-four hours a day, seven days a week. The flights were scheduled so close together that if a pilot missed his pass at Templehof Airport, he pulled up, got in line and flew the eighty-minute trip back to Frankfurt to get in the inbound line again.

When the Russians saw the Allies were not going to abandon Berlin, they finally decided their efforts to isolate the city were ineffectual. Early in May, 1949, they announced the lifting of the blockade and began to let supplies move again by surface transportation.

Seaboard was proud of its contribution to the Berlin Airlift, and rightly so. Considering what a small company it still was, the recognition received from the Air Force and War Department on both sides of the Atlantic was gratifying. Seaboard's president informed his people that "(our) participation in the North Atlantic portion of this lift was greater than any other single carrier in the United States."

By 1948, the exploding air transport business had necessitated the expansion of airport facilities in New York. Seaboard had earlier moved its operations from MacArthur Field on Long Island to LaGuardia Airport. Now, it was the first cargo airline to move from LaGuardia into the new facilities at Idlewild. (This is the same field later renamed John F. Kennedy International Airport.)

On July 1, 1948, the Port Authority of New York announced the opening of the new airfield. The following day, as Joe returned from one of his regular flights to Frankfurt, Germany, he expected to go into LaGuardia as usual. Instead, his landing instructions were changed and at two fifty-five that Friday afternoon, he landed the first plane from overseas at Idlewild, beating a Peruvian plane in by thirty minutes.

When the Halsmers had returned to Indiana and built their new home, the Berlin Airlift had only begun. With Seaboard pushing their pilots to the limit in the Berlin effort, Joe had scant time to give to the care of his five acre plot. In the summer of '48, the grass and weeds grew wild. The former pasture, now unrestrained by the trampling or feeding of stock, needed mowing. But little by little, the Halsmers accumulated equipment and began to turn it into a beautiful home for their growing family. The large yard was a blessing and soon the children would be big enough to help with much of its care.

On October 2, the third son, Cornelius, with dark hair and dark eyes, was born. Once again, Halsmer was notified by phone in a far city of the birth of his child.

The following month, a most unusual flight occurred. Seaboard contracted with a syndicate of American horse breeders to bring a race horse to a stud farm in Kentucky. The horse, bought in Paris, was Djelal, a famous champion, and worth $225,000.

In spite of the fact that this horse had flown across the channel several times for races, there was trouble getting him aboard. He was extremely nervous and high-strung, and when the trainer walked him up the ramp, the horse refused to lower his head to enter the opening. Several times he bumped his head on the doorframe, and it was fully thirty minutes before he was finally safely in his stall.

As the plane climbed out from Orly Field toward the 12,000-foot cruising level, the horse continued to show increasing signs of distress. He kicked and threw himself around in his stall as though he were in pain. The trainer, Jack Hare, was unable to calm him.

"Could we land? The horse isn't looking too good," Jack asked anxiously, poking his head in the cockpit doorway. They had only been in the air thirty minutes.

Studying their position, Joe found that the nearest place they could set down would be Bovington Airport in Herefordshire, England. It was another hour of flying even to Bovington.

Joe went back to see for himself what was going on. The horse was kicking frantically, out of control. His hooves were tearing at the padding on the walls around him, and in spite of a hypodermic injection from the trainer, he continued his violent actions. The restraining rope by which he was tethered finally broke and he threw himself to the floor of the stall.

There were seventeen crated dogs aboard that flight as well, and their furious barking added to the general commotion.

In a short time the handler administered a second sedative to Djelal in an effort to calm and control him. He seemed a little weaker, but still panic-stricken. Joe knew they had to get the horse on the ground, and he began his descent to Bovington. While they landed, the unfortunate animal slumped feebly in his stall and lost consciousness. When the plane came to a stop, ground crews carried the limp body out, and within a few minutes, he was pronounced dead.

It was sad to see a fine animal come to such an end, especially when it was so unexplainable. The handlers insisted he had often traveled by air in the past and had always adjusted to the conditions well.

One of the first things Joe did upon landing was to report to his operations officer at Seaboard and Western Airlines in New York. When he explained what had happened, the man in New York expressed regret at the unfortunate incident. Then, quickly, he asked: "Look at the airway bill, on that line where insurance coverage is indicated. Is that square checked?"

Sure enough, there in its little spot was that $225,000 check mark, to the great relief of the bosses in New York.

As Seaboard grew, there were frequent changes and shifting of personnel. Shortly after the Halsmers moved back to Indiana, Seaboard had offered Joe the position of chief pilot. The duties included supervision of all pilots and occasional line flying, as well as an increase in pay. And it would mean moving back to New York.

This position was essentially a buffer between management and the pilot group. Joe figured it would require even longer hours away from home and family than his present position of flying the line. He much preferred flying to supervising and settling differences. He and his wife gave it serious consideration, and he chose to remain in the flight section. His seniority as pilot number four gave him almost always his first choice of routes to fly, trip scheduling, and vacation times. He loved the work he was doing and had no desire to get bogged down in a combination of paperwork and office politics.

As it turned out, in a short time, more management changes came about and he could possibly have been squeezed out of the company. But as a senior pilot, his position was secure.

In the early days, Seaboard was certificated to fly only as a non-scheduled cargo airline. The pilots operated on an "on-call" basis. Joe never knew, when he returned from a trip, what day he would be called to go out again. His time at home might be two days or ten days, only partly depending on the demands of the air freight business. Other factors that governed his flights were the number of flying hours of his previous trip and the number of flying hours he'd already accumulated in that quarter of the year. Later, Seaboard was certificated as a scheduled line, and trips were bid and awarded according to seniority on a monthly basis.

Joe's family was accustomed to the uncertainties of his comings and goings, or, at least, he thought they were. Maybe it was harder on them than he realized. Years later he began to understand a little bit of what it must have been like. They never knew when he would be home for Christmas, Thanksgiving, someone's birthday, a daughter's slumber party, or a son's basketball game. Joe loved his wife and children very much, but during those years, perhaps he loved his flying a little more. He treated his crew members like family. When a trip departed one Thanksgiving Day, he arranged to have turkey dinners on the plane for his surprised and grateful crew.

In March, 1949 Joe left New York on what proved to be the most memorable trip of his career. It began when the cargo department in New York onloaded the heaviest and bulkiest single item yet carried. It was a 10,000-pound steel rudderstock for an oil tanker that had run aground in Singapore. Also aboard this flight was 5,000 pounds of boiler pipe for a freighter that had blown its boilers in the Persian Gulf.

They flew to Gander, Newfoundland, for fuel. Then on through Shannon, Ireland; Rome, Italy; and Cairo, Egypt; to Bahrain Island, where the disabled oil tanker waited. With three pilots, an engineer, a navigator, and two radio men, and with bunks on board, this crew could fly many hours without interruption for rest. Up to now, they had made good time, stopping only for fuel and offloading.

Now while the boiler pipe was offloaded, the crew took twelve hours of much-needed rest. Incidentally, they all got miserably sick for a few hours on bad food, but when it was time to leave for Karachi, all were ready to go.

At Karachi, they refueled, and as they took off for Singapore, oil and smoke poured out of the number one engine.

"Trouble, trouble! Now how long will we be delayed?" Joe loved to fly and he loved to work on engines—but when he was trying to reach a destination, he was impatient with delay. Reluctantly, he feathered the propeller and returned to land.

Down on the ground, as Joe examined the engine, he found it had burned up a piston. Engine parts had fallen into the crankcase, ruining the engine until it could be completely overhauled.

At this time, Seaboard was not a big airline. They had accumulated ten DC-4s and were doing well, but they did not have a stock of parts or even offices out in the far corners of the world. Joe took his crew out from New York with his pockets full of traveler's checks and it was his responsibility to accomplish whatever had to be done to complete the haul.

Stranded now with an unusable engine, Joe walked through the hangar of Pakistan Airlines, searching for an answer to his problem. Against the wall, he noticed an engine with some cylinders missing from it. It was a Pratt and Whitney, the same kind of engine as the damaged one in his ship.

When he inquired about it at the PakAir operations office, he was told it was sidelined with high time on it, waiting to be overhauled. Joe knew that job could be done only in the United States, an expensive proposition for PakAir.

"How would you like for us to take that engine back to New York for you at no charge?" he asked hopefully, with rising excitement. And he offered them a deal. The Seaboard crew would transport the engine back to the States in exchange for its use en route. It was agreed.

Joe and his men quickly got busy. They took the two good cylinders and pistons off their blown engine and put them on the PakAir engine. Soon it was running like a top. Then, with the job nearly complete, the engineer's face showed disappointment.

"We can't use this engine," he mourned. "The gear shaft boss for the Seaboard tachometer can't be fitted to that engine."

Evidently PakAir used a different type of tachometer. The Seaboard tach demanded a small recess for the gear shaft boss, and there was no such recess on the PakAir engine.

Joe had never forgotten his Pop's words: "If you can't do something it's because you haven't tried hard enough."

"Go get some supper," Joe told the engineer. "You need a break."

He hustled over to the big KLM shop and borrowed a drill and a steel bit with which he made the needed hole. When the engineer returned from supper, the engine was ready to be installed.

Removing the ailing engine and installing the substitute one was no small matter, but with the use of a chain hoist and a tripod, the job was complete in three days. This crew of seven had changed engines in less time than the same job usually took a maintenance crew in New York! They disassembled their own engine, stored it in the belly of the ship, and took off for Singapore.

Incidentally, these PakAir DC-4s had often been appropriated by the Pakistani government for use as bombers in their dispute with India. They would simply roll bombs out the back door over whatever target was chosen. The Seaboard crew was extremely fortunate that some unseen problem didn't afflict this engine, but once installed, it gave them no trouble.

The trip to Singapore was uneventful. When they arrived, the ship owner provided a construction crew with a large crane to offload the rudderstock.

This proved to be quite a job. The unloading crew, willing and able, was familiar with the heavy-duty equipment used around ships, but inexperienced with aircraft and unaware of how easily the structure of a plane could be damaged.

Joe and his crew worked with them for a long time to see to the protection of their plane. For instance, before allowing this unwieldy piece to be moved, Joe took precautions to see that at no time did its total weight rest on a single spot. With its weight so concentrated, it could easily break through the flooring. As it was moved to the back of the plane, it was necessary to protect the fuselage from the stress of bending. They winched the nose of the plane to a heavy truck to relieve the tendency to buckle the fuselage at midpoint, and to prevent the nose from rising as the weight was shifted. They added bracing under the tail to prevent it from being pushed down. And the door frame had to be protected as the heavy weight was eased through it. All in all, it was a tedious affair, but with care and the help of that heavy crane, it was done.

After the offloading was complete, Joe received a message from the home office. Right there at Singapore were some circus animals waiting to be brought back to New York. They took on crates carrying 116 noisy, smelly monkeys and a twenty-three foot python snake. The snake had eaten seven chickens and could be expected to sleep in his comfortable basket for a couple of weeks.

In addition, at Bangkok, Thailand, a shipper had four leopards and two golden cats crated and ready for loading. And there were six young elephants, each of which weighed 1,500 pounds.

As mentioned, Seaboard at that time did not have operations offices or service departments scattered throughout the world, so, as Joe managed the engine replacement in Karachi and the difficult unloading in Singapore, it was also up to him to attend to the necessary details for this shipment.

Protection of the plane from damage was always primary. This time it would be protection from the unusual cargo itself. The interiors were nicely appointed with carpeting on the floor and upholstery on the walls and ceiling. Since flights alternated between passengers and freight, the seating was constructed on rails. Seats could be slid out of the plane and stored in the belly whenever the load to be carried was freight.

In Bangkok, Joe bought canvas with which to line the floor. Then they screwed rings through the canvas into the floor so each elephant could be tied by one leg.

The weight and balance statistics of an aircraft are carefully calculated to produce safe flying characteristics. It would be a challenge to immobilize this moveable cargo of such huge individual sizes to prevent their upsetting this balance factor of the plane. Little did anyone anticipate what a problem that would become!

But first they had to get them aboard.

The cages of the two golden cats were covered. They were vicious little animals and would snarl and strike through the bars if the cover was lifted. But setting their cages aboard, and those of the leopards, was easy.

For the elephants, airport personnel built a long ramp out of teakwood. (Later, the crew joked that it might have been wiser to have brought back the teakwood and left behind the elephants, but that was hindsight.) They laid bamboo grass up the ramp to entice the elephants to eat their way into the plane. All worked well for the first five animals.

The last to move forward was the smallest one. He turned out to be the boss of the bunch. He herded the others ahead of himself and took his own time about joining them. When he was halfway up the ramp, Joe and the crew, impatient with all the time being taken for loading, decided they would "chase the little fellow" the rest of the way into the plane. He promptly lifted his head, turned, and chased them back off his ramp, and it took another six hours for him to eat his way, all by himself, into the plane.

Joe thought they were ready to go, but the elephants seemed uneasy and restless. Finally someone realized that the odor of the python might be the cause. A snake is one of the few natural enemies of an elephant. They moved the snake in his basket into the belly storage area of the plane. With its annoying scent gone, the elephants seemed more comfortable. The python rode to New York, cold, but safe down below.

Accompanying the animals was a young woman who had purchased them and was responsible for getting them to her buyer in New York. However, she seemed inexperienced with regard to handling elephants and was afraid to get close to them, so the crew ended up doing much of the animal care.

Joe stationed two men in the back of the plane with gas dipsticks to distract the animals, if needed, and began taxiing down to the end of the runway. He was running up the engines when there were frantic calls from the rear of the plane.

"One of the elephants is loose!" someone shouted.

They certainly couldn't fly under those conditions, so Joe taxied back

The Seaboard crew that changed the engine in record time in Karachi and brought back the elephants from Singapore: top to right, Captain Halsmer; Radio Operator Boyd Higley; Junior Captain William Donahue; Engineer John Zittere; Co-pilot James McCormick; and, bottom left, Radio Operator George Forero, 1947.

to the ramp. This time they rethought their whole containment plan. Using plywood and bales of straw, the men now built bulkheads. Untying the elephants, they simply confined them to a very small area.

Then they took off for Calcutta, Karachi, Bahrain Island, Cairo, and Geneva.

Although Joe had taken pains to protect the plane's floor surface, there was unanticipated havoc. The upholstery of the walls and ceiling was unprotected and at the mercy of their four-legged guests who had no respect for the decor. In their boredom, their restless trunks roamed everywhere. They pulled at whatever they could reach, and long before the flight reached New York, they had ripped and shredded much of the wallcovering, causing hundreds of dollars worth of damage to the plane's interior.

This concerned the crew, but another matter was an even greater source of anxiety. The elephants discovered that when they pushed against the wall of the fuselage, it gave, to some extent. This delighted them, but to the crew, it was disconcerting to see the fuselage bulge when one of these huge animals exerted pressure.

"Hey, guys, take it easy," cautioned one of the men, trying in vain to distract them with the dipsticks. "This airplane is the only one we have up here in the sky!"

With genuine alarm, everyone hoped the plane would hold together until they reached New York. It was a long trip home.

Then another problem arose. The monkeys were happy with their bananas and there was still some meat for the cats, but the elephants had eaten their way through almost all of the deep layer of grass brought for them. Soon they would have to take on some hay.

And there was still another matter. The gross weight of the plane would have to be reduced, but Captain Halsmer had no intention of shoveling manure for Seaboard. Dependable, obliging, he was always more than willing to do whatever was best for the company. But he had left the dairy farm to fly and he had no intention of returning to one of the farm's least attractive jobs.

So he called ahead to Henry Heguy for help. Henry, the station manager at Geneva, appreciative of the crew's predicament, took his responsibilities seriously. He had the good fortune to locate a vacationing Hagenback Wallace circus man who was willing to come out to the airport and give whatever assistance was needed. While he took care of things aboard, the crew got some much needed rest. The circus man knew how to handle animals. Once Joe saw an elephant try to pin him to the wall with his head. He simply batted the animal in the eye with his hand and the elephant backed off.

Joe was still concerned about the stress to the fuselage, so, at Geneva, he and his crew strung barbed wire along the inner wall of the plane to keep the elephants from pushing against it. They were becoming anxious to get this troublesome cargo home. As they left Geneva and headed for Iceland, they discovered that the wire, while it might have solved the pushing problem, infuriated the elephants, and they began bucking each other. They were like bored kids, scuffling simply for the

Rudderstock for the STANVAC CALCUTTA being offloaded very carefully to avoid plane damage at Singapore, 1947.

sake of activity.

Flying along at 10,000 feet, the crew was getting desperate. They were running out of ideas about controlling their unusual passengers. Then it occurred to Joe that perhaps a slight oxygen deprivation would calm things down a little. He knew humans could stand to fly at 14-15,000 feet without oxygen. Maybe these large animals would be affected at a lower altitude.

He climbed to twelve thousand feet and, sure enough, the lack of oxygen made them sleepy and weak. They all lay down and the balance of the trip was peaceful and uneventful.

The arrival at Idlewild caused a lot of excitement. Planes, now, were no novelty, but shipping large animals aboard them was.

Seaboard milked all possible publicity offered by the unusual cargo and arranged to have the news media present. The unloading attracted much attention because the elephants were as uncooperative at leaving their temporary home as they had been on entering it. They obviously didn't like the look of the ramp they were expected to walk down. (Probably they preferred teakwood.) People from KLM, Air France, and

The 'Singapore Trader' on the ground at Geneva, Switzerland, on the long trip home. Yes, that's an elephant getting some fresh air while his DC-4 gets refueled.

other airlines gathered and offered suggestions. Three of Seaboard's vice-presidents and the chief engineer appeared and tried to throw their weight around, but the elephants were not impressed.

Eventually, after six hours of coaxing and wooing with water and hay, someone thought of peanuts. A vending machine was found and a little bag of peanuts interested the first elephant in trying the ramp. After he worked his way slowly down, within thirty minutes all six of them were in the waiting truck, ready to leave for their new home.

The publicity Seaboard received from this exotic cargo was most welcome. Surely the newspaper headlines about the animals would open the minds of new shippers to the almost unlimited potential of delivery by air. In the company's early days there had often been uncertainty about the new venture's chances for ultimate success. Sometimes there had been barely enough funds to continue. On one occasion all of the pilots had agreed to a payroll delay so that no one would have to be laid off. But the management continued to be aggressive in seeking new business and now the future looked more promising.

At home, the airport business was doing well. The flight school was approved for veterans' education under the GI Bill of Rights. Many young men and women took advantage of that governmental assistance to become professional pilots.

As dealers, Halsmer Flying Service had on hand a Cessna 150 for instructing primary students, as well as a 172 equipped to teach instrument and night flying, and radio work. With the AT-6, they had done some air ambulance work, but they were unsatisfied with that plane for that job, so they acquired a twin-engine Cessna with space enough to carry a stretcher.

Shortly after acquisition of the twin, a tragic accident occurred at a Purdue basketball game when a large section of bleachers collapsed. Many people were injured and over the next few weeks and months, the Halsmers were able to be of help with their stretcher-carrying plane. Several people were flown away for specialized attention to their injuries, and many, still recuperating, were returned to their home communities faster and in gentler fashion than an ambulance could offer.

Aerial advertising was a good source of income for Halsmer Flying Service, too. They had upgraded their banner and now had very good materials for that profitable work. As it advertised various products, that banner was a familiar sight over Purdue football games for many years.

Several local businesses had begun to appreciate the advantages of flying their executives wherever they had to travel in the course of their work. Some owned their own planes and simply hangared them at Halsmer's, buying gas and using the maintenance facilities. Others contracted to pay a flat monthly rate for a specified number of hours of flying time in a Halsmer plane, with a pilot furnished. It was convenient for these firms to use this credited time as they needed it.

All in all, life was beginning to take on a little more security for Joe's family. In February, 1949, the firstborn son, Joey, turned six years old, so when September rolled around, there was some excitement as the first child left home for school. However, Josephine had little time to notice one less child at home. The couple was expecting again, and on January 27, 1950, Patrick was born. Now three-year-old Marianna had four brothers.

During Joe's time at home, he learned that the Purdue University Men's Glee Club had been invited to sing in July at the International Music Festival in Wales. Following that, they were to perform in several cities of western Europe. When Joe learned that their travel arrangements were still incomplete, he inquired if they would be interested in making their flight on Seaboard. Acting as agent, he was able to get the contract for Seaboard, and was assigned to be their pilot.

For some time Joe had wanted to take his wife to Europe and, finally, on this occasion, things fell into place. He got permission to sign her on as stewardess (the position later called flight attendant), and they hoped to have a few days layover together in Europe.

The UC-78 twin engine Cessna was an excellent plane for charter ambulance service, 1955.

The Glee Club consisted of fifty-seven young male students and a staff of twelve, including a couple of accompanists. They took a train to Washington, D.C., where they sang for President Harry Truman. The next morning, the Seaboard plane was waiting for them at Dulles International Airport and they boarded and began the flight north.

At Gander they landed for fuel and that included refueling the passengers also. When fifty-seven handsome young men walked into the terminal restaurant for a bite to eat, they attracted attention. People soon learned they were a singing group, and after their meal it didn't take much to persuade the genial group to entertain briefly with an impromptu songfest. The Halsmers' Hoosier hearts swelled with pride when the boys finished up with rousing choruses of "Back Home Again in Indiana" and "On the Banks of the Wabash."

After refueling again at Meeks, Iceland, the group arrived in Paris on a bright sunny afternoon. There was a band out on the tarmac and a conspicuous number of dignitaries around the offloading area.

"What a welcome this Purdue Glee Club has rated," the Halsmers thought.

Then they learned that Emperor Haile Selassie of Ethiopia was expected at any moment and the French government officials were there to meet him.

Joe confirmed his date with the passengers for the return trip out of London on July 10 and said goodbye to them. After finishing the paperwork, the crew gathered in the airport restaurant for a bite to eat and then went to the hotel, where Josephine got a taste of airline humor.

As the crew stood at the desk registering for their rooms, the Irish co-pilot, with a straight face, quipped, "I suppose the Captain gets the stewardess, as usual."

By eleven o'clock the next morning, the couple had eaten breakfast, strolled down the Champs Elysées, looked at the Eiffel Tower, and Josephine had had a glimpse of Paris. Joe needed to check at the hotel to see if there was a message from the home office. Yes, there was. Instead of the three- or four-day layover he had been given to expect, the crew was to report to Brussels, Belgium immediately. At eight that evening, they would return to New York. Ordinarily, Joe would be happy with such a quick turn-around, but now he had his wife with him, not waiting at home.

However, there was nothing to do but give up the hotel room, grab a taxi, and head for Brussels. It was a pretty ride through the French countryside. In Reims, they stopped for a quick look at the famous old cathedral with its beautiful rose window. By dusk they were at the Brussels Airport, and at 8:00 P.M. were ready to take off. It was a short vist to Europe for Josephine, but Seaboard wanted this plane and crew in New York immediately, and Joe would soon learn why.

CHAPTER 8

GOING STRONG AT 40 — KOREAN AIRLIFT

Greenland cargo drop—Gander weather emergency—Halsmer Airport vs. Purdue University Airport

N orth Korean troops had poured over the border attacking South Korea and the United States took police action against the aggressors. As usual, the military called on commercial aviation for assistance and Seaboard acted quickly when notified of the need.

Captain Halsmer hurried back to New York from Brussels that night, and with twelve other Seaboard pilots, was put to work in a full-press effort toward what was already being called the Korean Airlift.

Josephine hated to see her husband go to the Orient. His flying to Europe had become familiar, and therefore bearable. But as the responsibilities of their family had continued to increase, seeing him go twice as far away made saying goodbye twice as hard. However, in this instance, they had no choice. For that first trip west, Joe was to meet his crew and plane in New York. So he told his wife he would try to "buzz" her when he flew across Indiana. They both knew his buzzing days were past but he was able to notify her approximately when he expected to fly over their home.

It was cherry time in Indiana and that day Josephine had obtained a large supply of the fruit to freeze for pies for her growing family. She was sitting on the patio pitting the cherries when she heard the plane coming. Joe brought the powerful DC-4 down to 1,200 feet and the lonely wife shed a few tears into the cherries when he roared overhead and quickly disappeared off to the west.

At Fairfield Suisun Air Force Base, just outside of San Francisco, Joe's plane took on a load of bazooka ammunition and flew to McChord Air Force Base in Washington state.

When they stopped for fuel at McChord, they learned that although the military had a dozen DC-4s there on the field, not a single one had yet taken off for Korea. As the weeks and months went by, many troops were funneled through McChord. But at this point, the urgent need of the South Korean forces was for ammunition with which they could resist the Russian tanks pouring in from the north. Joe's load of bazooka ammunition was some of the first to reach the South Koreans from America.

En route to Tokyo from McChord, the flights fueled at Anchorage, Alaska, and Shemya, one of the westernmost islands in the Aleutian chain. There, Joe found the weather to be almost as nasty as that he had encountered over the Hump. The extreme updrafts and downdrafts were missing, but a heavy fog blanketed that area almost constantly as the cold air of the Arctic mixed with the warmer air moving north with the Japan Current.

The first time Joe tried to land at Shemya, he had to make three passes across the field. Heavy snow was falling, the ceiling was fifty feet, and the wind was blowing at sixty knots. With great relief, he finally got it down. As they taxied in they saw half a dozen wrecked aircraft of different kinds along the sides of the runway.

"Any landing you can walk away from is a good landing," say pilots fondly. They made a good landing.

It was very cold there, even in the quarters where the crew took their rest, but they were so tired they managed to sleep in spite of their discomfort.

From Shemya, they took off for an airbase by the name of Masawa on an island off the northern tip of Japan. This leg of the flight was a "sweat job" for several reasons.

First, it took them within 175 miles of the Russian-controlled coast of Siberia. Although the United States was not at war with Russia, it would be unwise to get too close to her coastline, especially while carrying supplies to her enemies.

In addition, there were no radio navigational aids along this coast, from 200 miles out of Shemya until they were within 150 miles of Masawa. Their ADF was useless. They had the wind drift indicator, and at night could take star shots. But the winds were strong and gusty, often consistently up in the forty to fifty mile range and above. With such winds and the constant fog, it was difficult to keep on course and avoid straying over the sensitive Russian territory.

For many months following the Korean outbreak Seaboard kept Joe assigned to flying the trans-Pacific trips, and the Purdue Glee Club singers returned to New York with a different pilot.

In June, the Halsmers' sixth child was due and Joe had bid for his month of vacation at that time to be with his family. In the first week of June that year, the temperature in Indiana climbed into the ninety degree range, and it stayed there for two weeks. Joe had always promised himself a swimming pool if he ever had the space for one.

Now, he decided, was the time to begin. He got a stake eighteen inches long and in the middle of the back yard he drove it into the ground. He tied a piece of twine to it, pulled the twine out to the end of its twenty-one-foot length, and there he placed another stake. Using this length of twine for the radius of his circle, he began digging a trench as wide as the spade and two feet deep. This was to be the footing for the outer perimeter of the pool. And it was the hardest labor of the whole project.

Friends who visited during this time jeered at Joe as they watched the sweat roll down his face.

"There are cooler things to do than digging in this heat," they said.

But his eyes were on his goal. When the trench was complete, Joe ordered a load of premixed concrete delivered and directed the driver to fill his circular earthen form. A couple of days later, with the concrete well hardened, he got his tractor out of the shed. Using its front scoop, he removed all the dirt from the center of the circle.

The pool was to be a modified cone design with a three-foot-wide band inside the perimeter. The center would be six feet deep and the outer band about two feet deep all around. This shape was Joe's design to protect small children from a fall into deep water. (Years later, with grown children around, he would build a two-foot wall atop the outer circle to deepen the whole pool.) After the cement work was complete, he also fenced off a portion of the shallow part for the little ones' swimming area.

He was well into scooping out that center dirt when, on June 23, another son, David, put in his appearance. Maybe he was anxious to get in on the swimming pool construction.

By the time Joe had the center all cleaned out, his vacation was over and he had to make another trip. But that would be an interruption of only a few days. He wanted the newly-shaped surface well packed, so he encouraged his little ones to do all the running they wanted on the temporary dirt floor.

As it happened, that trip turned out to be a return to the east, and an interesting one at that.

The crew, consisting of two co-pilots, two engineers, a radio operator, a navigator and Captain Halsmer, departed New York for Iceland. There, they were to pick up supplies for a French expedition doing geodetic work in Greenland. The group was studying the thickness of the ice cap in an attempt to learn the altitude of the land under the ice. Everything they were using needed replenishment.

At Iceland, Joe met a representative of the group, who had packed 10,000 lbs. of tractor parts, drill parts, fuel, and food into five-gallon fuel cans. He wanted these to be dropped at the work site on the ice cap at 5,000 feet above sea level. He gave Joe the north and south coordinates of camp's location.

Before the flight departed Iceland, their workers built a ramp in the plane from the rear cargo doors across the fuselage. They removed the doors and set in place a plywood piece which covered the opening on the inside. When the time came, members of the flight crew would pull this plywood aside to allow cargo to slide out. After all this preparation, they packed the cargo in the remaining space.

For the French, of course, there had to be wine. That, with some other goodies, was to be dropped separately by parachute.

Joe and his crew departed Iceland early in the morning and flew across the North Atlantic, approaching the east coast of Greenland at 12,000 feet to clear the mountains.

Because there were no radio facilities anywhere in the area, the only navigational aid available was the sextant with which the navigator could take sunline position shots. This is a procedure which would give them a line of position, but would not locate them on that line. (At night, two celestial bodies can be used to give a fix, a definite position. But in daylight with only the sun available, only a line of position is attainable.)

The navigator did excellent work, but they were flying in and out of cloud, and that hampered his calculations somewhat. He kept taking sunline shots, and when he estimated they should be about over the group, they were again in clouds and could see nothing. It would be dangerous to let down, because they had no way of knowing the altitude of the ice cap at that point.

The expedition was supposed to have on hand a manually-operated radio transmitter from which the plane could receive signals on their ADF, but in spite of continued calls sent out from the plane, they heard no answer.

According to the data given, the position of the expedition was about two-thirds of the way across the Greenland ice cap from the east coast where Joe's crew had begun their search.

Joe was concerned about his diminishing fuel as they continued flying without contacting the party. He decided to go west across the ice cap to the opposite coast. If the overcast there was broken, maybe he could identify surface features.

This proved successful. Over the west coast, they broke out of cloud and were able to identify Disco Bay. From there they dead reckoned back to the coordinates they had for the group.

At that point, again clouds restricted their vision. Joe called repeatedly on the radio and finally got a weak response.

Maintaining voice contact from that point on, Joe was able to find the object of his search. It worked like the children's game: "Button, Button, Who's Got the Button?"

"Tell me if the engine noise you hear is getting louder or weaker," Joe said to the man on the ground.

"It's getting louder! It's getting louder!" he continued, until finally, "No, wait! Now you're starting to get weaker."

"I'm going to make a ninety degree turn to the right," Joe told him. "Keep monitoring my sound."

From the responses then, Joe was able to close in on the exact position of the party on the ground.

The voice below said it was clear beneath their estimated ceiling of 2,500 feet so Joe asked him to shoot off a flare. When the crew could see a red glow in the overcast, Joe lowered the nose of the plane and they broke out of the cloud. There, right before them, was the camp of the expedition.

Joe slowly reduced his altitude and the crew began to load cargo on the slide. As they flew about fifteen feet above the snow, Joe waved his hand from the cockpit and his crewmen pulled the plywood away from the open door. The drums went tumbling out.

After all had been offloaded, Joe climbed back to 2,500 feet as instructed and threw out the specially-packed parachute containing the wine. Sadly, the chute failed to open, and the contents of that package were smashed.

The main cargo was retrieved from the snow in good condition, so the crew felt they had made a successful drop, but the wine drinkers may have disagreed.

When Joe returned from this trip, he was ready for more work on his swimming pool. For reinforcement of the pool floor, he bought steel wire and rods, and ordered enough concrete to pour it four inches thick. The first load of pre-mixed cement was to arrive in the morning at seven. It would be a long day.

Johnny was there to help, and Joe's sister, Evelyn. Joey and Pete, at eight and seven, were good workers. They had done some of the trench digging and had helped their dad shovel much of the dirt from the center. Marianna at four, and Neil at three, were helpful in keeping Patrick, the toddler, out of everyone's way, as well as running into the house often to check on baby David. Josephine was prepared to provide easy-to-eat food whenever the workers could take a break. Everyone worked steadily under the pressure of getting the concrete poured and finished to a smooth surface before it set. It all went surprisingly well, an exhausting but satisfying day.

Building the swimming pool turned out to be one of the best things Halsmer ever did for his family. All the children gained lifetime enjoyment of the water after learning to swim at the age of five or six. Throughout the summer months, many family parties and good times with friends centered around the pool. When the summer warmth gave way to the chill of winter, the children watched the dropping temperatures closely until the ice was hard enough for a good hockey game. Those were busy days, the seasons rolling quickly past.

Two years later, another baby! Finally, a second daughter, Joann, was born on June 24, a beautiful addition to the family.

Shortly after her birth Joe made his first circumnavigation of the globe. He left New York with a load of mixed freight, making fuel stops first in Goose Bay, Labrador and Shannon, Ireland. He dropped off freight in Frankfurt and Stuttgart, Germany. Then on to Cairo, Egypt; Basra in Iraq; Bahrain Island in the Persian Gulf; Karachi, Pakistan; and Calcutta, India. At Calcutta, instructions from New York ordered him to proceed to Singapore. From there he flew to Manila, where he picked up a load of over 1,900 monkeys for the National Polio Foundation for use in their laboratories.

At this time, polio danger was at its height in the United States. Researchers were frantically working to learn how to grow live polio virus, a necessity for the development of a protective vaccine. The kidney of a monkey was found to be the only culture in which this could be done successfully. In response to the demands of research groups, for several years, planeload after planeload of these animals came in from the Philippines, India, and the Malayan Peninsula to the United States.

On this trip, having approached Manila from the west, Joe's flight continued eastward. Through Wake Island and Honolulu, he returned home, completing his circling of the earth.

During all those hours in cockpits over India, while World War II was in progress, and later, over the Atlantic, as he flew for Seaboard, Joe had visualized many specific ideas about aircraft improvement. Now in his days at home between trips, he began to turn his ideas into something practical. With the large maintenance shop facilities of Halsmer Airport and a variety of tools at his disposal, he was at his happiest as he fleshed out his sometimes radical concepts.

In the early 1950s, he built a lifting body sixteen feet long, four feet high and eight feet wide. This is the maximum road width allowed. The intent of this design was to provide a vehicle for transportation in the air as well as on the ground. Some people call such a vehicle a roadable airplane, but Joe used the simpler term, aircar. Joe equipped his lifting body with a 155 HP Franklin engine and a Hartzell propeller. He built it by hand, riveting sheet aluminum to the angle aluminum he used for shaping the structure.

For lateral control purposes, on each side, he designed an eight-foot wing which had a five-foot chord and he equipped it with ailerons. When the aircar was to be driven on the ground, the wings could be folded back alongside the body.

On each side of the rear, there was a fin and a rudder for directional steering in the air. Across the top of the two fins was the stabilizer to give pitch stability. Attached to the rear of the stabilizer was the elevator for attitude control.

The prop had a reverse pitch which could be used to move the vehicle forward or in reverse. In his search for control, comfort, and firm steering on the ground, Joe first used a tricycle landing gear with a nosewheel. This proved unsatisfactory and he turned to the pontoon-style gear, which he later patented.

Joe and his brothers towed this model with a car in order to check its stability in the air. In several runs down the field they were able to get it off the ground. Its handling was satisfactory, but they quickly found that it was being adversely affected to some extent by the turbulence of the air behind the auto. So they hooked it behind an Aeronca Sedan, and Johnny towed Joe off the ground to an altitude of about 200 feet.

It flew so well that Johnny reduced the power of the towing plane. That was a mistake. At the slower speed, Joe's vehicle immediately began to sink. As he lifted the plane's nose in an effort to maintain altitude, the changed attitude increased his drag. Johnny's tow plane didn't have enough power to overcome that and Joe knew he had to let go. He looked quickly for a field in which to land. Releasing the trip rope, he dropped the nose in an effort to give himself some airspeed. As he neared the ground, he was able to flare out and land it in a hayfield with no damage.

The first 'lifting body' Joe built in 1954 sported a 155 HP Franklin engine mounted on top with a Hartzell propeller.

That test told Joe the body needed reshaping. He needed to decrease the depth in order to minimize drag and make it more efficient. And it certainly needed double the power for better performance. Like many creative-minded people, Joe was more interested in proving what he believed about the general idea than in its marketing. It would be an expensive machine to develop. And he had other experimental ideas he wanted to work on.

But Seaboard's scheduling office kept interrupting him.

In a 1954 expansion of their operations, Seaboard abandoned the faithful old DC-4s, and purchased their first Lockheed Super Constellations. The "Connie," affectionately nicknamed by her appreciative pilots, was a beautiful bird and carried up to eighteen tons. The cargo cabin's capacity was over 5,000 cubic feet. It cruised at 260 miles per hour and featured a wider than usual landing gear. Its three rudders and tailfins were a lower profile than most tail configurations and gave it better stability in crosswind situations than almost any other plane. It was a delight to fly.

With the Connies, the company continued to bring in a steady flow of monkeys for the research laboratories producing polio vaccine. The loaders packed those crates of animals into the fuselage as high as they could stack them, leaving barely enough room to walk down one side of the main cabin.

Even with the ventilating system going full blast, the odor from all

Joe began flying the SuperConstellation, Model 1049, one of his favorite planes in December, 1954.

those warm little bodies was incredibly foul. Since the humidity was extremely high, moisture condensed everywhere in the cabin. In the cockpit, brown droplets of water formed and dropped from the instruments over the heads of the crew. Often, several dry cleaning operations were required to remove the odor from the men's uniforms.

Arriving in New York after one of these trips, Joe was conscious of the scent clinging to his clothing as he boarded the TWA flight from New York to Indianapolis.

On a seat in the row in front of Joe, there was a carton of some kind, and he noticed the stewardess looking and sniffing every time she came near the area.

"My goodness," she finally said, "I hope there's not something rotten in this freight package. It sure smells bad."

At that point Joe thought he had better "clear the air," so to speak. And he told her he was to blame for her concern.

"I just got off a flight from India," he said. "For the last two days, I shared my Super Connie with a load of stinking monkeys, all for the good of mankind, of course."

She was relieved to know the offensive odor was not her responsibility and Joe was relieved that TWA allowed him to remain in their nice plane.

In the summer of '56, Mark was born, the third dark-haired baby, like Pete and Neil, and with the complexion of his mother.

The Halsmers enjoyed their eight children and were proud of them. All except the baby had chores to do around the place. They fed and watered their pets, and helped their mother with jobs in the house. By now, the older ones were caring almost entirely for the yard and the swimming pool.

Joe taught his sons, as soon as they were big enough, how to handle a tractor and a lawn mower. And when each one was big enough to sit on a pillow and see through the windshield, he had him or her in a plane handling the controls. Joey, the oldest, was already anxious to reach sixteen so he could solo. The older boys were also beginning to help their dad on his experimental projects.

Joe's life had achieved a wonderful balance between the challenge and excitement of international flying, the contentment of his home and family, and the satisfaction of his creative urges in his experimental workshop.

The aircraft of the day had become a highly developed technological marvel with wonderful capabilities. However, there was still one uncontrollable factor to which it was subject in a large measure. That factor was the weather.

On one occasion, Joe had picked up a load of monkeys in India and was making a normal return via Bahrain Island in the Persian Gulf, Athens, Rome, and Shannon, Ireland. Out of Shannon, the flight had passed the point of no return (the point at which the fuel supply will no longer return a flight to its departure point) when they received a report of deteriorating weather at Gander, Newfoundland. The field was closed because of eighty knot winds, gusting to 100. Off to the west, neither Stephenville, nor Argentia, an occasional alternate, was open to transit.

With all these fields closed down, Goose Bay, the only alternate

Joe's children enjoy the 'little car' he built for them. Left to right, the children are Joann, 3; Neil, driving, at age 8, with Marianna, 9, ready to go for a ride. Pete, age 12, fine tunes the engine while Patrick, 6, and David, 5, help Joey, 13, refill the thirsty gas tank. 1956.

remaining open, was crammed with the westbound traffic of every other airline off the North Atlantic. When Joe contacted Goose Bay, they told him they could not service his plane because of the congestion. If he landed with such dismal prospects, their cargo of monkeys might freeze while they waited for fuel. Goose Bay radio made it clear that they had no protected hangar space available.

Joe decided he could accomplish more at Gander than at Goose Bay, so he headed there. As they approached, airway control informed them that their staff had abandoned the control tower when high winds had blown the windows out. The runway lights were also out. It was 2:00 A.M. and this flight planned to land, refuel, and go on to New York.

There was an old range station at Gander, one leg of which was positioned over one of the runways. When Joe crossed the range station, turned and began to descend, he could barely make out the snowbanks on either side of the runway in the faint moonlight coming through the overcast.

The ceiling was 200 feet, and the winds were blowing at eighty to 100 knots straight across the runway. With equal portions of sliding and prayer, they made it.

They taxied up to the gas pumps, and when the ground crew tried to service the plane, one man was blown off the wing. Joe arranged to meet the gas tank truck on the downwind side of a hangar in order to receive the fuel they needed.

While the ground crew fueled the plane, Joe and his co-pilot went in to the weather office to take care of their paperwork. On the way in, they noticed a couple of military cargo planes parked with their tails into the wind, looking mighty vulnerable.

They mentioned the danger to some Air Force officers inside, and suggested that they might save themselves some damage if they would turn the planes' noses into the wind.

Later they learned their warning had come too late. Both those military planes were at Gander for months afterward being repaired. On each plane, the rudder was blown around the tailfin, and the elevator wrapped around the stabilizer.

If Joe and his crew had landed at Goose Bay, they would undoubtedly have had a long frustrating delay and probably a load of frozen monkeys. Many planes were on the ground there for days. Although the rough takeoff at Gander gave the crew some anxious moments, they got into the air safely and arrived in New York without the loss of a single monkey.

The Super Connie was a great plane for this kind of work. The lower profile of its tailfins and rudders, together with its long nose, gave it less tendency to weathervane, an excellent handling characteristic in a crosswind situation. Joe had to admit he probably couldn't have done it in his beloved old DC-4.

Joe's return home was even more joyful than usual after an exhausting experience like this. But after a night's rest, he was ready to work on another one of his ideas.

Over and over in his mind, Joe studied the dilemma of how to get twin-engine reliability within single-engine price range for the average private pilot. With all his traveling to far places in the big planes, when he was at home, he and his brothers flew Cessna 150s and 182s, an Ercoupe, and other light planes. Although improved technology and materials had upgraded the quality of engines by now, the unreliability of those early engines was still burned into his memory. It had been so commonplace to lose power and be forced to land that Joe always tried to make sure there was a clearing somewhere he could glide into. In single-engine planes, he avoided flying over large bodies of water and he taught his students and his children the same kind of common-sense flying. In his midwestern area, cutting across the southern edge of Lake Michigan tempted many, but not Joe. He loved to swim, but he never wanted to do it from a sinking airplane.

He began to consider how he could place two engines within the nacelle of a plane and somehow power each of the two props individually. Finally, between trips, he began working it out, and after many months came up with the Halsmer Safety Twin. Around home they called it the pancake twin because one engine was placed flat on top of the other as closely as possible. The top engine was inverted, the carburetor was relocated to a position between number two cylinder and the fire wall, and a new intake manifold was built. With these changes, Joe could "pancake" the engines very close together. The crankshaft of the upper engine was extended twelve inches, and the prop for this top engine was mounted directly on this extension. Behind this front prop, on the shorter crankshaft, the second prop was mounted with bearings. It was connected by four v-belts to a pulley on the bottom engine. The two props mounted in this manner on the shaft and its extension operated completely independently of one another by way of the belts.

Joe built this configuration into the nose of three different planes with a useful increase of power and only a slight increase of drag. The result was a twin-engine design that coped with the failure of either engine with complete directional stability.

The first test ship was a 120 Cessna in which Joe installed two 80 HP Continental engines with two McCauley propellers. He put many hours of labor into this plane and was pleased with its performance. He worked with a patent attorney in Indianapolis and eventually was awarded a patent on this engine installation.

It was time to approach manufacturers about its marketing. Howard Piper of Piper Aircraft was interested, and he commissioned Joe to build this configuration into a Piper Tri-Pacer which Piper provided. Joe spent several months completing the job, and Piper was happy with the finished product.

But Piper Aircraft had expected to use this work in a new plane to be built mainly of plastic. When their new model proved disappointing, they cancelled its production and were unable to use Joe's design.

The business at Halsmer Airport was growing well. At this time, they operated one of the largest flight schools in the state. They offered a complete charter service for businessmen, doctors, farmers, and others, and, with the twin-engine Cessna, ambulance cases. All hangar space was rented.

In 1955, Halsmer Flying Service added to its facilities an eighty-by-100-foot metal building with a door across one end giving thirty-foot clearance. They moved their maintenance shop into this building, and also hangared larger planes in it.

The first model of the Halsmer Safety Twin (top) was the Cessna version in which Halsmer replaced an 85 HP Continental engine with two 80 HP Continentals. In the Tri-Pacer he modified for Piper Aircraft (bottom), he replaced the 150 HP Lycoming engine with two 100 HP Lycomings. 1955/56.

That same year, it was evident that a more substantial runway was needed to accommodate the heavier usage.

With persistence, they found a highway contractor who had the equipment for this kind of work, and it happened that right then he had the time to do the work. He had a big job coming up in the near future and didn't want to lay off any of his workers. So Joe and his brothers made a deal with him. The Halsmers would furnish the fuel for his equipment and pay the salaries of his men if he, in turn, would level the ground and prepare it for runway paving.

Meanwhile, the flying brothers also traded a local asphalt company an airplane at cost for installation of an asphalt runway at cost. The airport ended up with an excellent paved runway at a very reasonable price.

The Halsmers knew the value of the good black Hoosier loam they had removed for the foundation of the runway, so they instructed the construction men to stockpile it off to one side. Over a period of several years, they supplemented their income with its sale to local nurseries and other interested parties. The brothers always looked for ways to earn an extra penny whether it involved flying or not.

In the late 1950s, the federal government made funds available to local communities for purchase or development of airport facilities. Lafayette citizens were interested, so the Greater Lafayette Chamber of Commerce appointed a Board of Aviation Commissioners to consider the matter.

Ever since the Purdue University Airport had opened, it had developed and grown, and the university furnished its students a fine education in aviation. They also offered instruction, charter flying, and aircraft maintenance to the general public.

The Halsmers contended that the university, operating as a non-profit educational institution from a tax-free base, competed unfairly in the aviation business when they aggressively extended their services outside the student body.

Purdue Airport and Halsmer Airport were, at that time, the leading airports of the area. When the question arose as to which of the two sites might be best suited for further development into the main community airport, a lengthy controversy ensued.

Halsmer Airport offered a longer runway with excellent approaches. It also had the advantage of being situated on high, flat, unemcumbered land on the growing side of the city.

The Halsmers presented a proposal to give their land to Tippecanoe County for its use as an airport, with the stipulation that Halsmer Flying Service be designated the fixed-base operator. This would enable the county to apply to the federal government for funds matching the valuation of the airport, estimated at the time to be about $325,000.00. These funds could then be used for improvement of the runway and development of terminal facilities.

Purdue University wanted their site to be considered for community use, but was hampered by legalities that would not permit the university to enter into a lease agreement with the county, or in any way to turn control of the airport over to anyone outside the university.

With numerous meetings and full media coverage, the controversy continued over a period of many months. But life went on in the Halsmer household, and on August 26, 1958, Robert, another fair-haired son, arrived in the family.

Finally, a bill was presented to the state legislature to enable the university to circumvent their legal restrictions. The Halsmers' fight against this legislative action was supported by many other local citizens, and the proposed change in the law was defeated.

At that, Purdue announced its intention to expand and develop without county or federal funds.

On May 2, 1960, the Tippecanoe County Board of Aviation commissioners declined further consideration of Halsmer Flying Service's offer to the community.

So for another 27 years, the Halsmer brothers operated one of the few privately-owned, full-service airports in the nation.

CHAPTER 9

HONORS AT HOME —
VIETNAM AIRLIFT

The aircar and safety-twin awards—
Snipers at Ton Son Nhut Airport, Saigon

Still looking for a marketable vehicle that could be flown for long distances and then driven on city streets, Joe worked at refining a second model aircar.

One prominent concern was twin-engine safety with single-line thrust, but fully as important was a method of keeping the wings with the vehicle when it was on the ground. For the first objective, Joe installed engines both front and rear in a push-pull configuration. Then he devised a means of folding the wings back along each side of the vehicle, locking them into position in a simple, yet strong and secure manner. Unfortunately, it quickly became obvious that for surface travel, the front propeller was dangerously exposed. Reluctantly, he eliminated it and worked only with the pusher propeller which was well protected between the folded wings.

For a good landing gear, he improved the four-wheel pontoon-type gear he'd used earlier. This gave him an undercarriage stable enough for highway speeds that could adjust to the attitude changes of the fuselage in takeoffs and landings. A patent search revealed nothing like it on file, so he got it patented.

While he developed these details, he also tried to interest a manufacturer in financing the certification of his design. In order for a plane to be offered for sale to the public, its design must be approved by the

The earliest model of the 'push-pull' aircar was built in 1958/59 with 75 HP McCullough engines in the front and rear. The original version had a nose wheel. Its folded wing design was strong, secure and quickly reversible. Pictures show both positions of the wing. 1958/59.

Federal Aviation Agency, a very expensive procedure.

Joe invited a representative of the Cessna Aircraft Company to evaluate his machine. The Cessna engineer came and after they inspected the aircar, Joe showed him a movie film that demonstrated its flying

In Model 2 of the Aircar, Joe removed the front engine with the exposed puller prop, judging it to be too dangerous. He replaced the two 75s with a single 85 HP Continental in the rear where, in surface travel, pedestrians would be shielded from it by the folded wings. Model 3 sported a pontoon shaped gear, a great improvement over the nosewheel. 1960/62.

characteristics. They viewed these pictures together, and on the same reel, there were some shots of the earlier model on which Joe had used the two engines in the push-pull configuration.

This was the design Joe had discarded because he considered the forward prop a danger on the ground. The Cessna rep asked question after question about the details of this model and when he left he was non-committal about any future interest. Joe heard no more from him. However, about two years later, Cessna put on the market their push-pull twin, the Skymaster, which they promoted very successfully. Of course, in a plane instead of an aircar, the forward prop had all the advantages and none of the exposure problem which caused Joe to discard it from his aircar design. Joe discussed the matter with the Cessna people, but he had no legal protection for his design, so it ended there.

In January, 1960, a third daughter was born to Joe and Josephine. Maureen was another dark-haired hint of the Irish side of the family.

Later that spring, then-Senator John F. Kennedy visited Halsmer Airport during his campaign for the nomination to the Democratic presidential ticket. He came to Lafayette for a dinner and rally at the local high school.

With great enthusiasm, the men strung their tow banner from one telephone pole to another, proclaiming: "WELCOME SENATOR KENNEDY." The family decorated the cart of the children's pet burro with red, white, and blue crepe paper, and the children were present in it to greet him when his Convair landed. As Senator Kennedy stepped out of the plane, his eyes caught sight of the banner and he broke into that familiar grin. After he had met the local dignitaries, the senator stepped over to the cartful of eight children where Joey was holding Isabelle, the burro.

He smiled widely and asked, "Is this all of you?"

"No, the baby, Maureen, is asleep in the office," one of the children answered. Upon learning the Halsmers were the parents of seven sons and three daughters, he chatted briefly with them about the joys of a large family, then proceeded into town for the rally.

With so many of the family responsibilities resting on Josephine while he traveled all over the world, Joe tried to treat her to a holiday whenever he could. He knew she'd been disappointed ten years earlier when their trip to Europe was cut short by the Korean Airlift, and he wanted to try again to take her on a European vacation. He also wanted to buy a diesel car. Seaboard offered its people low-cost shipping on a space available basis, so Joe arranged to purchase a Mercedes and have it shipped home from Germany.

On the day of their arrival in Frankfurt, Germany, Joe and Josephine took delivery of their car. They drove it down to Heidelberg for a bit of sightseeing. Then, so the car would be in New York before they returned, they turned it over to the Seaboard representative at Frankfurt for shipment home.

The vacationing couple spent several days in Rome, and the highlight of their trip was a visit to St. Peter's. Along with a large crowd of German pilgrims, they had an audience with Pope John XXIII, truly a memorable occasion. But the real climax for Joe came a little later.

Joe had first visited Rome back in the forties, and at that time, he had had an audience with Pope Pius XII. He and his co-pilot were part of a group of only fifteen admitted at that time. Though Pope Pius was reserved and quiet, Joe was impressed with his friendliness, as he spoke with them in English about their flying careers.

Pope John was a different kind of person. He was less formal, as he laughed and dialogued with the large group of German-speaking people who filled the hall. Though the numbers involved were much greater,

When then-Senator John F. Kennedy was campaigning for the nomination for the presidency in 1960, he came to Lafayette for a rally, landing at Halsmer Airport. The Halsmer family greeted him with Isabel, their pet burro, pulling their gaily trimmed cart. At left are Halsmer and Senator Kennedy. The children in the cart are, left to right, Robert, Joann (hiding Neil and Patrick), Mark, Marianna, and behind her, David. Josephine stands at the right. Behind the cart, from the right, are Police Chief Harold Swick, Mayor William K. Gettings, Harold Kull, Theodore J. Smith, James Murtaugh, and Councilman Al Gillis, all of Lafayette; Robert E. Peterson, Rochester; Lyndall Wilson, Kokomo; and between Kennedy and Halsmer, Alex Hanewich of Wheatfield.

and though Pope John spoke no English, he still conveyed a warm sense of his love to all.

The audience ended with a blessing and the Halsmers began the long walk out of the building, striking up a conversation with a woman nearby.

She seemed interested when she learned that Joe was a pilot. Then she revealed that she was the youngest daughter of Louis Bleriot, the French pioneer aviator, first man to fly the English channel! She said she had lived in America for many years, married an American, raised her family there, and had become an American citizen. She was in Europe to see her mother.

Joe was delighted to meet someone so close to one of his beloved heroes of early aviation! He especially enjoyed asking her questions about her childhood and her father's early flying activities. For Joe, that was truly memorable!

Following their papal visit, the couple took a train from Milan back through the Alps to Zurich, and flew home from there. It was a wonderful vacation, and when they reached New York, the car was there, ready for them to drive home to Indiana.

In 1961, Seaboard again upgraded its equipment with six brand new CL-44 models of the Canadair. It was one of these planes, manufactured in Montreal, Canada, in which the frightening electrical failure occurred. On that same flight, the crew had encountered other serious problems that were unrelated to the electrical system.

When they had taken off at Frankfurt, Germany, for the return trip home, they headed for Lakenheath, England, where they were to pick up a military load. Soon after they were in the air, Halsmer had trouble moving the ailerons. As the flight proceeded, they became increasingly difficult to activate, By the time the plane was over Brussels, there was no aileron control at all. Halsmer had to keep the wing level by varying the application of power to the outboard engines.

This procedure was especially difficult in this plane. Its low-wing design lacked the necessary dihedral angle (upward slope of the wing from fuselage to wingtip) to give the plane natural stability. Its instability was heightened by the placement of most of the weight of the fuselage above the wing. This plane required constant work from the pilot to keep it flying straight and level.

In attempting to compensate for the loss of aileron control with engine power, the stage was set for dangerous possibilities. The slightest overpower to either engine could begin an oscillating action that might be impossible to stop. The sensitivity required here would be difficult enough in level flight. To turn or to attempt landing with such marginal control would be extremely precarious.

They were approaching London where the runways were wider and longer than those at their destination, Lakenheath. So at 10:00 PM, Halsmer called London radio and declared an emergency. He requested permission to come straight in on runway twenty-seven. Air traffic control vectored him in to land to the west and they began their descent.

At 3,000 feet, the ailerons unexpectedly broke free!

Joe cancelled his emergency landing arrangement with London traffic control, got clearance to return to the airways, and the flight went on to Lakenheath, where they landed without incident.

Later they learned this problem stemmed from the Canadair's unique use of torque tubes for aileron control. Instead of the usual cables, aileron movement was controlled by torque tubes passing through the fuselage wall and into the wing through a snugly-fitted bearing. The plane had come through hard rain over Brussels and water had seeped onto that bearing surface. As they climbed into colder altitudes, this moisture froze and prevented all movement of the torque tubes. The warmer temperatures encountered as they descended thawed the ice-encrusted bearing and set the tubes and ailerons free. The manufacturer was forced to modify this as well as the electrical system.

At Lakenheath, while the military ground crew loaded the airplane, Joe filed his flight plan and necessary clearances. When the loadmaster reported the plane was almost ready to go, Joe began his usual walk-around inspection.

Before every takeoff, with a well-trained eye, Joe gave his plane a thorough visual check—the tires, the control surfaces, and the props. He looked for any possible damage that could have occurred during the plane's last flight or its time on the ground.

As he walked around the front of his plane, he was shocked to see the nosewheel strut fully extended. The tires were hardly depressed at all; the wheels almost off the ground. It indicated clearly to him that the plane was tail-heavy.

The ground crew was ready to move the heavy swing-tail and lock it into position, when he bellowed at them in a voice that left no doubt who was in charge.

"Don't move that tail! Don't under ANY conditions move that tail! You must have made some mistake in loading," he warned the men. "That plane is extremely tail-heavy."

And he cautioned them again against any movement of the tail section while he went to look for the loadmaster. If those men should move that tail into position, Joe was sure the whole rear of the plane would collapse to the ground.

The Candair CL-44 acquired by Seaboard in 1961. Lower photo shows the "swing-tail" open. Other planes took advantage of the tail-loading concept by designing the empennage (tail assembly) high enough on the fuselage to allow an access door beneath it.

He found the loadmaster in a nearby office, and told him there had been some mistake in the loading. But the loadmaster brushed him aside.

"There's no mistake. Everything is fine." He was so sure he and his men had made no error.

Finally, at Halsmer's insistence, he walked out and looked only at the back end of the loaded plane.

"There's nothing wrong with that load!" he repeated with the cockiness only a sergeant can muster.

"Look," the irritated Halsmer blurted, "You get your commanding officer on the telephone. I want to talk to him."

It was 2:00 in the morning and the sergeant certainly didn't want to wake up his CO with a telephone call.

But Halsmer refused to enter the airplane and returned to the office where he asked the director of operations to call the commanding officer. The captain dialed the phone and handed it to Halsmer. After a couple of rings, the colonel in charge of the base answered.

"My plane that your men loaded is off balance," began Captain Halsmer. "But your loadmaster insists it's okay and won't correct the matter. I refuse to take off in it. I want you to come out here and look at the situation."

At the words, "...you...come out here and look..." the colonel was more wide awake than he wanted to be.

"Let me talk to the sergeant," he said gruffly.

They talked briefly and Halsmer heard the loadmaster say, "Sure it's correct, sir!" before he handed the phone back.

The colonel expected to close the matter here and now.

"If my man says the plane is loaded correctly, it's loaded correctly. I'll assume full responsibility for it."

Halsmer didn't care how willing the colonel was to "assume full responsibility." It was his own neck that would be sticking out if he tried to take off in that tail-heavy plane.

He was not unfamiliar with that kind of situation. Some of the early plane designs had been heavy in the tail. If a plane is even slightly tail-heavy, the stick may go forward almost all the way to the stop before the pilot gets the desired response of a lowered nose. It is a mighty uncomfortable situation for the stick to be jammed forward against the stop and have the nose argue with the pilot about whether or not it will go down. If the pilot can't get the plane's nose lowered, the plane will simply lose its forward speed, the natural law of gravity will take over and the plane will fall from the sky, tail-first. Under some conditions, a plane can be brought out of a tailspin, but generally, it's impossible to regain control of the craft.

The barnstormer in Halsmer didn't want even to think of such a possibility in that huge, heavily-loaded plane. He could feel his face burn as the anger rose up inside him.

"Colonel," he charged ahead, "You say you're willing to be responsible. Good! You get your ass down here right away and look over this situation for yourself. I don't intend to move this airplane until it's loaded properly."

When the loadmaster heard a civilian speaking to his boss in that way, he decided maybe he should do some further checking about the numbers and weights of the pallets in the disputed plane.

These planes were loaded with numbered pallets. The weight of the freight on each pallet was noted. A chart is then drawn up suitably distributing the total weight so that the aircraft will be properly balanced within safe limits. The pallets were then to be slid into the cargo hold on rails, according to the chart.

By the time the colonel arrived at the field, the loadmaster had discovered there was indeed an error. In order to balance the load properly, every pallet had to be removed and replaced.

The repentant loadmaster was all apology. And the colonel was a perfect gentleman about it. He willingly notified Seaboard, as well as the military authorities, that responsibility for the three-hour delay was due only to the military people involved.

Seaboard was proud of its record for prompt deliveries and pickups, both for commercial work and for the many military contracts they flew. Naturally, they wanted any delays properly accounted for on the records.

It was following this late takeoff from Lakenheath that this same plane experienced its nearly tragic electrical failure. The CL-44s began their Seaboard service with several problems, but after they were corrected, the plane proved to be durable and dependable.

Another of Joe's experiences with the Canadair began in Spain. A planeload of military dependents had come in from Turkey and the debarking crew told Joe they had experienced an engine problem inbound but didn't know the cause.

Neither the mechanics on the base nor the technical representatives flown down from the engine manufacturer, Rolls Royce in Great Britain, were able to find the answer to the problem.

All suspected the fuel, but finally, without learning the cause of the trouble, Joe and his crew took off for the Azores Islands and Savannah, Georgia. At first, everything went well, but near the end of that long leg to Georgia, the engine began running rough again. However, they landed safely.

Joe then took the plane up to New York empty, but on that last leg, he had to feather the number two engine and fly the remainder of the distance on three engines. The conclusion was that the fuel was thought to have been contaminated by some kind of fungus growth, picked up from a tank in Turkey.

In 1962, Joe took his family to their first Experimental Aircraft Association International Fly-in at Rockford, Ill. The EAA is made up of people interested in and supportive of general private aviation. Many of them had built, or were building aircraft for their own personal enjoyment. Joe had joined the EAA when he began building his various experimental models. That first year he didn't exhibit a plane, but he and Josephine took all of the children except the two oldest boys, who were kept home by summer jobs. The family had bought a tent-camper the year before. So, towing it with their nine-passenger station, they joined the large segment of EAA members who camped for the week-long show. Six-month-old Dominic, their eleventh child, had arrived on February 28. By August, he too was old enough to go camping.

The display of all those home-built aircraft stimulated Joe's enthusiasm. He figured his ideas were at least as good as those being shown. After the air show concluded, he was anxious to get back to the airport and work on his aircar. But Josephine and the children wanted to extend the camping trip into upper Michigan. So they drove north enjoying the beautiful wooded area, until, halfway around the lake, the water began to look more attractive than the miles of highway ahead of them. They found a ferry that would take them across the lake and the boat ride was a nice change.

Camping blossomed into a good vacationing choice for the family. The following summer they went east for the children's introduction to the ocean. They included Washington, D.C., where they visited the senate and took a tour of the White House.

That November, when President John F. Kennedy died so tragically, the family's sadness was sharpened by their brief but personal memories of him.

In August of that year, Joe flew his Model 3 Aircar to Rockford, and Josephine drove the station wagon filled with children, towing the tent-trailer. This was the pusher model aircar with the pontoon landing gear. Displaying a plane that elicited so much interest was an exhilarating experience for Joe. People kept him busy all week answering questions and for a climax, EAA awarded him a trophy for the Most Unusual Design.

On January 20, 1964, another daughter joined the family.

Christine Marie arrived two weeks before expected. Again Joe was away on a trip, and Josephine faced alone the news that they were the parents of a Down's syndrome baby. Often these babies have a congenital heart weakness, but the doctors all said Christine's physical condition was good. Joe and Josephine, believing God had blessed them in a special way to entrust to them a child with special needs, took her home and cared for her.

In March, Seaboard took delivery of a fleet of Douglas DC-8 airplanes to replace the Canadairs. All the pilots to be checked out in the eight studied for two months at Douglas Aircraft in Long Beach, California. The ground school was hard work, but Joe enjoyed it. Josephine was grateful when, in the middle of Joe's schooling, a dear friend agreed to care for the children and she spent two weeks in Long Beach with Joe.

The 55 model of the DC-8 was among the first of the jet freighters. It cruised at 600 miles per hour, and its ability to carry an added 20,000 lbs. of freight at nearly twice the speed of former equipment was a big boost to the economic life of the company. It was such a well-designed and stable airplane, it was a pleasure to fly.

At this time, Seaboard had a contract with Trans Caribbean to fly between New York and San Juan, Puerto Rico. Joe flew many of these short jaunts. He would leave New York at 10:00 A.M. and return at 7:00 P.M., sometimes flying two or three trips back to back and staying in New York overnight, in order to decrease his commuting time.

That summer, after school closed in June, the family wanted to see the New York World's Fair. But Joe wanted to save his month-long vacation for August to attend the EAA Fly-In. So a compromise decision was reached. Joe would bring his family to the east coast, where they could camp and visit the fair while he made his San Juan trips as usual. The original tent-camper had been exchanged for a modified school bus with more sleeping room for all and a special spot had been arranged for the baby. But it was not to be.

In the midst of all this planning, it became apparent that Christine was not thriving. She was not nursing well and she stopped gaining weight. The doctors told the parents Christine's heart was not able to work hard enough for her small but growing body and said the prognosis was not good. In three short weeks after that dismal forecast, she was gone, one day before she would have become five months old.

The grieving family went on with their plans. While Joe made two San Juan trips and a three-day trip to Europe, the family took in the World's Fair and spent four days in a New Jersey campground, using Joe's four days off to return home. The children had many happy memories of New York and the fair but the parents themselves were glad to get home. It's said that one reason people enjoy camping so much is because home always looks so good when you return.

Joe was especially happy to be home again, working, between trips, on Model Number 4 of his aircar. Satisfied with the performance of his third prototype, he was determined now to build one that would not only fly well, but would be comfortable and attractive to drive. He was still flying Model 3 but Model 4 would be an all-metal four-seater with a 185 HP engine in it.

Neil and David gave their dad a lot of help in riveting, and when Joe needed someone to buck rivets for him in tight spots, he called on eight-year-old Mark.

At this same time, since Piper was no longer involved, Joe tried to interest the Mooney Aircraft people in producing his patented Safety Twin. He wanted to build the best prototype he could, and he believed the Pietenpol fuselage was the one to use. He located a wrecked one over in Champaign, Illinois, and he and Neil brought it home and began work on it.

That fall Josephine decided she wanted to learn to fly. After eight hours and fifty minutes of dual instruction, she soloed and did a fine job, loving every minute of it.

As the old year turned into the new, however, she began experiencing that old familiar nausea that told her another baby was on the way and she put her flying on hold for the time being.

These days, Joe's trips were mostly to Europe, with occasional short runs down to San Juan, and sometimes a San Juan trip back to back with a Frankfurt run. The increased speed of the DC-8 brought the New York to Frankfurt trip to a scant six and one-half hours, with the return trip taking eight and one-half, courtesy of the ever-present headwind from the west.

There had been some delay in getting enough crews checked out in the new DC-8s. As a result, often long before the end of any quarter of the year, Joe would already have flown the maximum number of hours allowed by FAA regulations. Then Seaboard would be forced to give him the rest of that quarter off. He might be very busy the first two months of a quarter, then have up to two weeks off until a new quarter began.

For some time Seaboard had also been flying supplies to Vietnam, with several crews based in the San Francisco area. Joe never considered moving, but now he wanted to bid for the longer trips across the Pacific in order to get more flying time per trip. As the fast DC-8 reduced his flying hours, his commuting was becoming a burdensome proportion of his time away from home.

Josephine hated to see him fly west again, especially before the baby arrived. She remembered the Korean Airlift and those ten-day to two-week trips.

But now the planes were faster, and every Pacific trip took more flying hours than almost any European trip. Therefore his maximum allowed flying time would accumulate faster and Joe could expect to have more time at home. So, in early 1966, they agreed to try this for a while and Joe flew west again.

Seaboard was carrying military troops and supplies to Saigon from Fairfield-Suisun Air Force Base just outside San Francisco. They flew either by way of Hawaii and Guam, or by way of Alaska and Tokyo, depending on where the weather was most advantageous.

It was seventeen and a half hours flying time from San Francisco to Saigon by way of Honolulu and Guam. Often they would return via Tokyo, five hours northeast of Saigon, then another ten hours back to San Francisco. They also flew into DaNang, Ben Hoa, Cam Rahn Bay, Clark Field in the Philippines, and Kyoto, Japan.

On September 9, 1966, Timothy was born, and with all Joe's traveling, he was there to greet him. Joey, now in the Navy, flew home from the Naval Air Station at Jacksonville, Florida to see his baby brother and his mom.

The following May, Joe's twenty-year anniversary with Seaboard came along but there was little time to celebrate.

The Vietnam War was not going well for the United States. The Viet Cong were shelling the airport at Saigon and Joe now came as close to combat flying as he ever cared to get. Some of his old barnstorming savvy came in handy. Once again he was landing with as steep descent as possible, cutting the power and dropping in as he had done in his old Taperwing when a field was small and surrounded by trees. But this time it was to avoid the tracer fire at the end of the runway, and in a very different airplane.

American helicopters hovered around the borders of Ton Son Nhut Airport, watching for ground fire from the snipers. Flares were constantly being sent up to light the whole area. And at a higher altitude, fighter planes were present to give protection from any possible air attack. It was like being in a movie, except that it was all very real, including the bullets, and Joe and his plane were in the middle of the action.

The presence of the helicopters unnerved Joe more than any ground fire. They operated completely without lights, and since they moved so much more slowly than the DC-8s, he feared running one down.

While his plane was being unloaded, Joe always examined the exterior carefully for bullet holes. Some Seaboard equipment sustained damage there, but throughout the many landings he made there under such conditions, he never found evidence of bullet damage on a plane he piloted.

In August, 1967, when second son, Pete, graduated from Purdue, he immediately joined the Army and prepared to enter helicopter school. Now there were two Halsmer sons in the service. Joey, a Navy pilot, had been assigned to the carrier Forrestahl, and was on his way to Tonkin Gulf to bomb North Vietnam. The war was quickly becoming a much more personal thing to Joe and his family. They mounted a map on the refrigerator door and kept track of the fighting as reported each day in the media.

August was also time for another EAA Fly-In. Each year the crowd arrived earlier and got larger. It was becoming more and more difficult to get a campsite close to the flight line where they all liked to be. With Neil and Patrick now responsible young men of nineteen and seventeen, Joe and Josephine decided to send the older children to Rockford three days ahead of their own departure date. They packed all their gear in the school bus camper and sent them off. Both boys could drive, and their dad knew they could take care of any auto problem that might arise. David was sixteen, and a good helper. Marianna was twenty and used to mothering her brothers and sisters, and Joann, fourteen, would keep her company. Josephine and Joe would follow soon with Mark, Robert, Maureen, Dominic, and Tim, now almost a year old.

This was going to be a great year at Rockford.

Shortly before leaving home on Saturday morning, Joe learned there had been a bomb explosion aboard the aircraft carrier Forrestahl. No one knew yet how serious the incident was, and Joe decided not to mention it to Josephine. He alerted a good friend at home and told him how to reach them at the air show.

The parents arrived at Rockford and found the older children well set up in an excellent campsite. The next morning they all drove into town in a friend's car to attend Mass, and Joe stopped for fuel before returning to the field. He bought a Sunday paper in the service station office and, without even glancing at it, he laid it, folded, on Josephine's lap. As he walked around the car and got in the driver's seat, Josephine opened the paper to see the glaring two-inch headlines about explosions and fire aboard the Forrestahl. The number of people dead and injured was as yet unknown.

It was a very bad time.

The accident was much worse than Joe thought from the first report. Josephine wanted to go home. But Joe convinced her they could be reached there at the show as easily as at home. So they stayed, and prayed. And they read the terrible news reports each day.

As word filtered back to the states, it was learned that the cause had been the accidental firing of a rocket from one of nine F-4 planes that were parked on the flight deck of the carrier. It had pierced the fuel tank of another plane, and fire and explosions followed. All nine aircraft on the deck were destroyed and nearly 200 men lost their lives.

As each day slowly passed with no word from their son, hope cautiously grew that the word, when it finally came, would be good. It was Thursday before the family knew that Joey was all right. Moments before the fire occurred, he had returned from a flight and was at the far end of the ship. But it had been a horrible experience, and some of his friends lost their lives.

Later, the Forrestahl slowly made its way back to Norfolk, and Joey was restationed at Jacksonville. He was fortunate enough not to have to return to combat.

The war in Vietnam kept getting hotter. On one of Joe's trips, he was held for three days in Guam because Tan Son Nhut Airport in Saigon was closed to civilian activity by intense enemy fire. Seaboard's last plane to get in and out before the airport was closed took eight bullet holes, thankfully none of them in a vital spot.

In between trips to Saigon, Joe built some refinements into his Safety Twin engine installation in his Pietenpol. One was a simple clutch that enabled the second engine to be started by the first one. It was a handy way to control the start from the cockpit and he got it patented. In the 1968 EAA Fly-In at Rockford, this model won the Best Engine Installation Award, given by Continental Engines.

Seaboard now took delivery on a newer and larger version of the DC-8 designated the 63 model, but widely called the "stretched eight." The fuselage of the stretched eight was thirty-six feet longer than the earlier model and had six additional feet of wingspan for improved lift. The four Pratt and Whitney engines produced 1,000 pounds more thrust, increasing the plane's range by 300 miles. Although its speed was not markedly faster than the '55 model, its greater payload of 107,000 pounds made it a very efficient plane.

Around this time, Pete completed his Army helicopter training. Joe never cared for choppers. He always thought if a fixed-wing plane vibrated as badly as the average helicopter, it would have been grounded. But Pete loved them. He finished first in his class and won the "Outstanding in Flight Achievement" Award. In return for all that expensive training, the Army wanted Pete to sign up for four more years of service. But he didn't love the choppers enough to extend his enlistment. So he refused and was ordered to report, after a four-day visit home, to McChord Air Force Base at Seattle.

That same weekend in Joe's first trip in the new stretched eight, he too was directed to McChord at Seattle. He was to pick up a load of troops and take them to Cam Rahn Bay.

Joe hoped Pete might be on his flight, but they learned later they'd missed each other by twenty hours.

Things turned out well for Pete, though. Because of his electronic education at Purdue, he was assigned to Can Tho, where he spent his year working on aviation electronic equipment in an air-conditioned van. During the time Pete was stationed there, Joe was able to call him on the phone a couple of times when he was on the ground at the Saigon

In August, 1968, Halsmer exhibited his Halsmer Safety Twin Engine configuration at the Annual Experimental Aircraft Association Fly-in and Convention. In a Pietenpol fuselage he had installed two 65 HP Continental engines and mounted two MacCauley propellers.

Here Continental Motors Director of Marketing Support Don Fairchilds, center, presents Halsmer, left, with the "Most Outstanding Continental Engine Installation" award at the EEA convention. At right is founder and then-president of EAA, Paul Poberezny. This photo used by courtesy of Teledyne Continental Motors General Products, Muskegon, Mich.

Airport. These were precious moments of reassurance to a father to be able to speak to his son in the midst of a war.

There were still occasional trips to Europe, too.

On Seaboard's first flight of a stretched eight out of Kennedy Airport, the payload was 107,000 pounds. It was thought to be a world's record for an aircraft crossing the Atlantic. Joe was excited about this distinction. Seaboard checked the records, and learned it was indeed a record weight for a heavier-than-air craft. However, the all-time tonnage record was 108,000 pounds, set in 1933 by the Graf Zeppelin. Hats off to the dirigible!

In the world of international cargo transport, there is frequently danger due to weather or mechanical problems. But sometimes danger comes from an unexpected source.

At home, Josephine read the newspaper headlines about a Seaboard plane being forced down and held by the Russians off the Aleutian Island chain. She knew that Joe had left New York several hours earlier, and was somewhere in that area. An anxious day passed before she was able to learn from Seaboard's operations office that a different crew was in Russian hands and Joe was in Japan awaiting that plane's arrival. He and his crew were scheduled to take it on to Saigon.

Because of the kind of flying Joe had done on different occasions, his background had several times been thoroughly investigated for security clearance. There was his involvement in the Berlin Airlift, the Korean Airlift, and now, the Vietnam Airlift. In addition, immediately after the war, he had commanded Seaboard planes that had flown politically-sensitive people out of Europe to various spots around the world by the arrangement of the State Department. And at the time of his discharge at the end of World War II, he had risen to the rank of major in the U.S. Air Force. All those factors colored Josephine's picture of what the Russians might do with Joe if he fell into their hands. Both were relieved that it didn't happen to him.

As it turned out, the Seaboard plane that was detained by the Russians was held for only a few hours and then released.

In the late summer of 1970, Neil was to receive his wings from the Army at Ft. Rucker, Alabama although he already had his commercial license. It was a family joke that, although Joey, Pete, and Neil were all accomplished pilots when they entered the military, the Navy, Air Force, and now the Army all "taught" them to fly!

Joe and Josephine decided it would be nice to take a little drive to Alabama and be present when Neil graduated. Included in their plans for this trip, after their visit with Neil, was a jaunt over to Monroe, Louisiana. There they would attend the convention of the Hump Pilots

In the mid-60s, Seaboard acquired a fleet of Douglas DC-8s, later upgrading them to the larger, so-called "stretched" 8s. "A beautiful, stable, easy to fly machine," according to Joe. This is the plane that served so well in the Vietnam Airlift.

Association, the veteran pilots who served in the China-Burma-India Theater during World War II. Joe had never attended one of these reunions and he was looking forward to seeing some of his old friends.

The visit with Neil was enjoyable, and when the ceremonies were finished, they headed for Louisiana. En route they visited a couple of little airports.

"You never know what you might find in someone's deserted hangar," Joe always thought. "Perhaps a forgotten old Jenny?"

Joe continued to nurse this fantasy that someday he'd find an overlooked treasure. Maybe that dream has something to do with the way he lost his own Jenny.

One day, back in the forties, many years after all had moved on to bigger and better planes, a man came by the airport and Joe chatted with him for a while. He showed the stranger his old Jenny, stored there in one of the hangars. The stranger said he had the facilities to restore Joe's plane for him and offered to do the job. They agreed on a price and the man took the plane home to Illinois to rebuild it.

After a considerable time passed, Joe inquired and was shocked to be told that a windstorm had come through the Illinois area and destroyed the Jenny. The fact that the stranger hadn't even bothered to inform him of his loss led Joe to question his honesty about the situation. There are several well-restored Jennies and Joe likes to think that at least some parts from his old plane may still be flying.

After an uneventful drive from Alabama, the couple arrived at Monroe. They checked in and learned that within the hour there was to be a boat ride on the Atchafalaya River, a sort of floating cocktail party. It sounded like a good place to find old friends, so they joined a group that was to be shuttled out to the river. They boarded the large river cruiser and headed up to the top deck to get something cold to drink.

With glasses in their hands, they had their eyes on an empty table ahead, when they heard a voice call out, "Joe? Joe Halsmer! Is that you?"

The three partners of Halsmer Flying Service, Inc. in 1970. Left to right are John, Francis, and Joe.

CHAPTER 10

CORRECTED HEADING

A new look at life, but still flying—Romania, Alaska and Guam incidents—A vision of Jesus—Stampe fun—the Holy Land visits

"**S**tew Lindke! I haven't seen you since we flew the B-17 up from Ponca City. What have you been doing with yourself since then? What a treat to find the two of you here!"

Stew and his wife, Cecelia, invited the Halsmers to join them. The women had met briefly once before, so as Stew and Joe talked flying, the women got reacquainted.

"Yes, we flew down here in the 310." Stew was enthusiastic about his four-place Cessna. "It's a fine plane. It gets me and my family anyplace we want to go. How about yourselves?"

"No, we're driving. You know the story about the shoemaker's children going without shoes. I always hate to take a plane away from the airport for fear my brothers may need it for a charter trip. Besides, I get in plenty of hours with Seaboard. We're flying Douglas stretched eights, the sweetest plane I've ever flown," Joe went on. "Seaboard's talking about getting some Boeing 747s, but I'll turn sixty in four years and be forced to retire in January of '74. I'll be lucky if we get them before that."

"It was a miracle," Joe heard Cec saying to Josephine, "how she got off those awful drugs." When Joe heard the word "miracle," he turned from Stew to listen to the women.

Cec continued, "It was because of the prayers of all those people."

"How did those two women get on the subject of religion?" Joe wondered to himself.

Seeing Joe's interest, Stew added to Cec's words: "Yes, our lives were completely changed by what happened to our daughter."

And Stew and Cec told how their daughter had been set free from drug addiction and returned to her family a few days after she was prayed for by a prayer group.

Josephine and Joe were both praying people, but they had never had prayer answered like this. They were interested. Every parent of teenagers worries about drugs. As the Lindkes spoke of all that had happened to them and their family, the Halsmers were struck by the deep joy that surrounded them.

The boat trip ended and the group returned to the motel. During the dinner, there were speakers, and there was some visiting with others, but after every interruption, the conversation between the Halsmers and the Lindkes kept returning to the answered prayers Stew and Cec had experienced.

Long afterwards, all Joe could remember was what happened when the four returned to the motel room after dinner. Cec picked up the Gideon Bible on the desktop and began to read from the Acts of the Apostles. It was amazing how fascinating it was. Joe and Josephine had tried to read their big Confraternity version of the Bible at home once or twice, but it always seemed so dry. When Cec read, it sounded like the story of real people, with God in the middle of it all.

"And our lives today should reflect that same interaction with God!" Cec was pleased at their interest. "Did you ever," she asked, "tell Jesus that YOU accept the gift He gave YOU when He died on the cross for you? Have you ever thanked Him for what He did for you?"

Joe had to think about that. He'd never looked at his religion in that way. His regular church attendance proved that he believed in God, didn't it? Or did it?

"On the other hand," he thought, "I guess people can attend church for many reasons. Do I only go to please Mom and Pop? Or out of habit? I'd always believed God was around when I needed Him, but otherwise, He wasn't really much in my thoughts."

The four of them discussed these things all weekend. During the two-day drive home, the Halsmers talked of little else.

"How come I had never thought of God in terms of how much He loved me? How come I was always more worried about whether or not I was displeasing Him?" Joe thought as he drove along.

The following week, as he sat in his cockpit en route to Vietnam, the engines droned away. The crew were all busy about their tasks. Joe's mind kept returning to what had happened during the past weekend, and what they'd read in the Bible.

"Everyone who calls on the name of the Lord will be saved." (Acts 2:21) That's what Peter told the crowd that gathered on the streets of Jerusalem.

"I've called on the Lord often," Joe reflected. "But I never knew I was saved. I thought that depended on how good I was. Is there something I've been missing up to now?"

It was time to get busy. They would soon be landing.

On some of the flights into Saigon, the cargo or troops were offloaded and the plane returned empty. But on other happier occasions, troops were waiting to return to the United States. And there were times when the men on active duty were to take some time off for rest and recreation.

This time at Ton Son Nhut Airport, a group of U.S. Air Force personnel were scheduled to go to Bangkok, Thailand on "R and R" leave. Joe noticed a general and several colonels.

They loaded without delay and took off, arriving over Bangkok with the ceiling at only fifty feet, but with the air smooth as silk. There was heavy ground fog and the runway was moist. Joe began his Instrument Landing System (ILS) approach at 2200 hours.

As they came down the glidepath, he reduced power gradually, never having to increase it. He touched smoothly onto the wet runway. He knew he had greased it in. It was impossible to tell when the wheels touched the surface.

After shutting down the engines, Joe rose and opened the cockpit door. The other crew members were getting to their feet behind him. The general in the first seat behind the cockpit looked up in surprise from the card game he was playing, as Joe stepped through the door.

"Where are you going? Aren't we landing?" he asked.

"We're on the ground," Joe told him.

"I can't believe we're on the ground!" he exclaimed. "That was the smoothest landing ever!"

"It got away from me," Joe smiled. "Before I got it under control, it slid in." It was good to have pilots aboard to appreciate a job well done.

Now Seaboard had an eastbound trip for Halsmer. It involved a load of 300 young beef cattle to be picked up in Chicago. In the main cabin, the shippers built a double deck arrangement and put 150 head on each deck. They headed for Bucharest, Romania, where the animals were to be used for breeding stock.

Thoughts about his relationship with God pervaded Joe's mind constantly these days. It was strange. Where formerly his thoughts had centered on airplanes, especially when he was flying, now all he could think of was Jesus. Stew had said the key to abundant life was each individual's commitment to Jesus.

"If you really believe," Cec had said, "that Jesus is God's Son as He claimed to be, then tell Him you want to belong to Him. God loves everyone, but He has special care for the people who acknowledge Him as their God."

"I guess I never thought much about whether or not I 'belonged' to God," Joe mused as he flew along. "I thought having faith meant I believed there was a God. I've been through some pretty scary experiences and I always believed He took care of me. But Stew and Cec spoke of looking for God's direction in all the decisions and choices of my life."

Now, Joe suddenly found himself seeing God's hand everywhere, in everything. But consult Him about everyday decisions? That was something else—a strange, but somehow inviting thought.

Everything went well with the cattle load until they reached the Romanian border. Joe had been assured that all the proper clearances had been filed for them to enter Romanian territory and land at Bucharest. Now, the Romanian radio was saying this was not so. Joe contacted Frankfurt radio and discussed the situation with Seaboard's representative, thinking he might have to double back and land there.

"Don't do that!" Seaboard's man knew the German regulations. "If you land here without the papers Germany requires, the authorities will shoot all the cattle!"

What a hassle! Joe felt caught in the middle. He was only the driver trying to follow orders, using up his fuel while people who were safely earthbound decided what he should do. Arguing over the radio with the Romanians all the way, he kept his heading for Bucharest and on arriving, he landed. For two hours the disagreement continued and officials refused to allow any of the crew to disembark.

Finally, not wanting to lose this opportunity to acquire good beef stock, they did offload the cattle. Some of the animals escaped during the unloading process.

"Serves them right!" Joe couldn't restrain some chuckles as he watched airport personnel chasing the animals with a jeep. Then he was surprised to find himself regretting such a mean little thought.

All the while, no one was allowed to go from the plane to the air traffic control offices. But the crew needed weather information and clearances to leave the airport. After three more hours of dickering, someone brought the papers out to the airplane. The crew completed all the forms for their departure route and taxied out to take off.

But Romania was not finished with them. As they sat at the end of the runway, the control tower delayed them yet another hour before granting permission to leave the ground.

When Joe got home from this tiring trip, Josephine was excited about a phone call she had received.

"Do you remember Don and Marilyn Miller, who learned to fly at the airport some time ago?" she asked him. "They've invited us to come to a Scripture sharing meeting in their home."

No wonder Josephine was interested. Since the Louisiana trip the couple had been reading a modernized New Testament called *Good News For Modern Man.* They enjoyed it, but so many questions came to their minds, they were attracted by the opportunity to read it with others.

"They called twice before. It was always on a night I had to take Mark or Robert to basketball practice. But this week, Wednesday was my only free night, so I went. It was great. Following the Scripture reading they pray for one another. They were all excited about a young man they had prayed for last week who had gotten badly burned rescuing a girl from an auto accident. They'd heard he was recovering surprisingly quickly. They pray expecting answers, like Stew and Cec!"

The following Wednesday Joe was home and able to attend also. Soon it became a regular occasion, meeting with these people who lived in and around the nearby village of Dayton. Week after week, as they read the Word, the excited couple began to see how often God speaks there of His deep love for His children.

Joe began to consider his own children and how well he had shown them his love. He and Josephine had talked of taking the family abroad but hadn't followed through. He would soon be retiring, and the reduced fare privileges he enjoyed through Seaboard's reciprocal agreements with other airlines might change at that time.

School schedules had to be accommodated, so Joe questioned the family about their interest in spending Christmas vacation in Hawaii. His question caused a lot of excitement. But he found that there were some other questions he should have asked first, like, "Can we get hotel reservations?"

With his earliest inquiries, he found that all hotels and all airline flights were booked solid. He learned that Hawaii is a popular vacation spot for west coast people.

David, at nineteen, was now the oldest at home. (Three weeks earlier he had enlisted in the Marines and was waiting to be called to boot camp.) Joann was seventeen, Mark, fourteen, and Robert, twelve. Maureen was ten, Dominic, eight, and Tim, four years old. Nine people to fly standby, over the holidays? It didn't look promising.

But a little persistence, with a generous helping of desire, paid off. (And what about those faith-filled prayers they were now praying?)

They learned that few people travel on Christmas Day, and they finally received a confirmation of rooms from a hotel. All the details were arranged. Then, on Christmas Eve, Josephine brought in the mail with a stricken look on her face.

"The Waikiki Outrigger Hotel has returned our check and says our reservation was a mistake. They're booked solid throughout the holidays. Now what? I'm not going halfway around the world with seven children and no hotel rooms assured!"

The Waikiki Outrigger had suggested another hotel, so by phone, Joe found another place that could handle all nine for Christmas night only, the night they expected to arrive.

Josephine was anxious about these incomplete plans for her brood, but Joe reminded her that Mary and Joseph had no reservations when they traveled that first Christmas Day. And Mary was pregnant. He also reminded her that he had traveled all over the world for years without reserving hotel rooms ahead and had never been at a loss for a place to sleep. Josephine thought finding a room for a single was quite different from finding rooms for nine people. But together, they decided to trust God.

At 3:00 A.M. on Christmas day, going straight from Midnight Mass, the ten of them piled into the big station wagon, already packed with suitcases. Patrick drove the travelers to Chicago where they boarded a PanAm 747 departing at 6:00 A.M. for Los Angeles and Honolulu.

As they flew west on a nearly empty plane, Joe recalled with satisfaction how good it had been to talk to his son recently. After Neil's graduation in Alabama, he had been sent to Long Than in Vietnam. On two different occasions, while Joe waited in Saigon for his cargo to be unloaded, he and Neil had been able to visit on the phone. Then, more recently, Neil had flown into Tan Son Nhut Airport in the Mohawk he used in his night reconnaisance work, and they'd had lunch together.

When the traveling family arrived on Oahu, they found the hotel a pleasant, comfortable place. And the management agreed to accommodate the family for the length of their stay. The beaches and the sightseeing were all they'd hoped. A side trip to Tahiti over New Year's weekend added a cosmopolitan flavor.

Joe had a few uncomfortable moments in Tahiti when he realized how far away he had brought almost all his family.

"What if something happened so far from home?" he wondered.

But then, if ever, was an excellent time to practice his new trust in God. The only alternative was to worry, and Joe had never considered worry productive. In spite of the spontaneity of the preparations, everything went beautifully. Nobody had to ride in the belly of the plane, and nobody slept in the street. Everyone had a wonderful time.

Some of Joe's ability to trust probably came from his mother's deep faith. When he and his brothers began praying and worshipping with non-Catholic Christians, she asked God if what they were doing was okay. One morning, shortly after, as she watched a news program on television, the picture being shown dissolved into the face of Jesus smiling directly at her. As she watched, amazed, He seemed to be assuring her she need have no concern about her sons' spiritual lives. She took it to be the answer to her prayer.

Joe's flights west continued. On one of his next trips through Tokyo, he met Fr. Bernardine Schneider, OFM, who was stationed at the Franciscan Center there. Fr. Bernie had been working in Japan for several years with scholars of different denominations translating the Bible into the Japanese language. He and another American priest, Fr. Stephen Lynch, found Joe's conversion experience interesting. When Joe learned Fr. Stephen was returning to America for a vacation, he invited him to come to Indiana.

By this time, the Halsmers were meeting with not only the Bible sharing group at Dayton, but with almost any other group they found that was worshipping Jesus. In addition to reading the Bible, they found other books that taught them more about the gifts of the Holy Spirit and their place in daily life. They read *The Cross and the Switchblade,* by David Wilkerson; *They Speak with Other Tongues,* by John and Elizabeth Sherrill; *Catholic Pentecostals,* by Kevin Ranaghan, and Steve Clark's *Spiritual Gifts.*

When Fr. Stephen came to Lafayette, the Halsmers took him to a prayer meeting at St. Tom's, the student parish at Purdue.

That evening, a young student delivered a prophecy in tongues, and a portion of it was in Japanese. When Fr. Stephen heard this unknown girl speak, in Japanese, an encouraging word about his work in Tokyo, he was astounded. At the close of the meeting, he went straight to the young lady to investigate. He was amazed to find that she had no knowledge of the Japanese language and had no idea she had spoken Japanese words.

Father Stephen returned to Japan with a new understanding of the Holy Spirit at work.

By now both Josephine and Joe had received the gift of tongues (praying and speaking in a language unknown to them), and were also experiencing occasional words of supernatural wisdom and knowledge. Joe had also spoken forth prophecies. St. Paul defines and explains these gifts of the Holy Spirit, and their use and benefits, in the twelfth and fourteenth chapters of his First Letter to the Corinthians.

Along with all the interest and growth in prayer in his life, Joe was still flying for a living and loving it.

Depending on the weather and the size of the load, Seaboard's westbound planes would fly either the northern route through Alaska and Tokyo, or southwest through Hawaii and Guam.

On the flights through Tokyo they used Cold Bay, Alaska as a refueling point. There was almost always ice on that runway. Workers spread sand to aid the plane's braking action, but only part of the problem was solved when the aircraft stopped.

Brakes always heat up, even in a normal landing. Then, as they cool down, the hot discs tend to stick to the brake lining if not properly ventilated. One reason the wheels of planes are routinely chocked upon parking is to allow the brake to be released, so the discs can cool in a separated position.

Often in starting, when the plane begins to move, a pilot may notice a "breaking loose" sensation as the wheel begins to turn. But a pilot cannot always be sure when he releases his brakes that the discs have separated.

On an icy surface, when the friction between the pavement and the wheel is not present to help the discs break free, this adhesion can become a hazard. The wheel can slide along instead of turning, and no one may be aware of it. Joe found that during the hour it took to refuel and complete the paperwork at Cold Bay, the brakes often baked together.

It was easy for this to go unnoticed when a plane taxied out. On the taxiway, where there might be no sand, a wheel could be sliding instead of rolling. When the runway was reached, the increased speed could damage the sliding tire. And if sand had been applied there, its abrasive action could quickly round off the bottom of the tire, causing it to go flat. The increased drag of the flat tire would retard the plane's speed, possibly to the point where the pilot, as he neared the end of the runway, could be moving too slowly to lift off.

Any or all of the eight main gear wheels could be affected.

When Joe became aware of this danger, he arranged for a signal from the ground dispatch personnel. From their position, they could see if all the wheels of a plane were actually turning. Later, white stripes were painted on the planes' tires to enable the ground personnel to be more certain of the turning of the wheels, especially at night.

The southern route to the west took them through Guam, a 212-square-mile dot at the end of the Mariana Island chain. Guam, 2,000 miles west of Honolulu, is an interesting place. But it's a tiny spot to find out there in all that water. Wake Island, off to the northeast, is a

God-given alternate. Wake is less than three miles square, but at least it's there.

Throughout the Vietnam War, a Russian radar ship was anchored about three miles off the west coast of Guam. The B-52s that were bombing North Vietnam were based on Guam, so the Russians continuously monitored U.S. activity there. Each time a flight of B-52s left on a bombing run, the Russian ship undoubtedly alerted the North Vietnamese.

But the Russian ship was not Joe's only memory of Guam. On one occasion, as he was preparing to take a DC-8 from Guam to Vietnam, an incident occurred which shows the immediacy with which a pilot must often make life or death decisions.

During the takeoff run, suddenly the stall warning device actuated. This is a mechanical attachment to the stick which warns the pilot if his speed is too slow for the plane to fly. The pilots' name for it describes its function dramatically: the stickshaker.

They were taking off to the west, and Joe had lifted the nosewheel off the ground, putting the plane into flying attitude (called rotation), when suddenly the stickshaker sent the stick into violent shuddering. It certainly snapped everyone in the cockpit to attention. Straight ahead, at the end of the 12,000 foot runway, was a sheer drop of 200 feet. Under normal conditions, the runway length was sufficient for their maximum load of 80,000 pounds.

Joe had seconds to make his choice: abort? or continue? He had seconds to wonder what his actual speed was. Was his airspeed indicator wrong? Or was his stickshaker malfunctioning? Should he attempt to abort the takeoff? COULD he stop the speeding plane before it got to the end of the runway? Would they end up trying to fly at the bottom of that 200-foot drop-off? Abort? or take off?

Many years of listening to engines, and particularly his familiarity with this plane, led Joe to believe his speed was adequate. He suspected, instead, a fault in the actuation of the warning device. But there was no time here to hedge, or weigh percentages, or second-guess his own hunch.

Quickly, Joe shouted for the engineer to pull the circuit breaker on the stickshaker.

The plane continued moving forward. They made a safe takeoff and there was no trouble of any kind with the engines. Joe's idea about the faulty stickshaker was correct. Again God had given him wisdom in a hazardous situation.

As Joe's recognition of his Father's protection intensified, he was not only speaking to Him more often in prayer, but also speaking of Him more openly to others, to any and all who would listen. He remembered reading: "Freely you have received, freely give." (Mt. 10:8) His crews began calling him "Preacher Joe," but he couldn't have cared less. Peter had spoken of wanting to please God rather than man, (Acts 4:19) and Joe wanted to be like Peter.

At one meeting with the Dayton group, several people asked him to pray with them for the Baptism of the Holy Spirit. (Acts 1:5, 2:1-4, and 19:1-6) After they prayed, all received the gift of tongues and some were overcome by the power of the Spirit and fell to the floor. (Scripture documents instances of persons falling under the power of God: Lv.9:24, Jg.13:20, Jn.18:6, Acts 9:4.)

One young man was delivered from a demonic attack. After writhing and twisting and kicking, as though in fierce anger or pain, and crying out unintelligibly, while the group prayed for him, he relaxed and became calm. He rested in the Spirit for some time and was allowed to lie there and wait upon the Lord. This deliverance was certainly a new experience for Joe and it came about quite unexpectedly. But God was true to His promise to be present and to protect those who put their trust in Him. This young man later was married and ordained, and is now pastoring a church on the east coast.

Joe was not alone in facing new experiences. The whole Roman Catholic Church was called to many changes when John XXIII convened the Second Vatican Council in October, 1962, for the express purpose of refining the work of the Church in ministering the Good News to the world. One of the results was a relaxation of some of the regulations pertaining to women in religious orders.

The Franciscan Sisters at St. Boniface were now living a more active life than before and it was an inconvenience to them to be without a car. The matter was discussed at a meeting of the Parish Council, then, between trips, Joe headed up a drive for funds for the Sisters' car. Parishioners responded well and soon the Mother Superior was given the keys to a new car.

In another instance, Joe worked with the parish in a situation that became ecumenical unexpectedly. This was some ten years before the Vatican Council urged Catholics to reach out to other Christians.

When the Halsmer children first entered school, a public school bus was available. It brought them into Lafayette to within a block of St. Boniface Grade School. Later, changes in the public school system eliminated that convenience.

To avoid having to drive the children back and forth to school each day, Joe bought a used school bus, contacted several families nearby with the same problem, and for many years, he and the neighbors operated a cooperative school bus route. (It was an old bus, and Joe enjoyed the challenge of keeping it running.) The families involved were happy to learn they could also include some children who attended two other Christian schools.

After twenty years of operation and several upgraded vehicles, the then-current bus was donated to the Lafayette Catholic School system, and for the first time, the system itself offered bus transportation to the families it served.

The above-mentioned Vatican Council was widely recognized as a work of the Holy Spirit. Joe found evidence elsewhere of that same work in many surprising ways and places as people came to new understanding of one another's beliefs.

One Mother's Day, the Halsmers were interested to hear a beautiful homily about Mary at a Methodist service. An unexpected and heartwarming surprise, it was all about how she should be honored as the Mother of Jesus.

On another occasion, one of these same Methodist friends had the Halsmers smiling as she shared that she had learned from Scripture that God had assigned an individual angel to every person for their protection.

"Marietta, we learned about guardian angels when we were children. The Catholic church has always taught that!"

In Joe there blossomed a strong desire to cooperate with this work of

The culmination of the drive for funds by the Nuns On Wheels Committee. Left to right, Al Bonner, Sister Katherine, Sister Theonita, Sister Eileen, Sister Juanita, Joseph Wilhauck, Halsmer, Keith Butz, and Herb May, 1976.

the Holy Spirit in bringing people to respect and love one another. He looked for specific things he could do.

The local Catholic high school was not being used to capacity, and Joe wondered if other Christian parents might be interested in sending their children to Central Catholic if they were invited to do so.

The Catholic schools have always been open to students who are not Catholic, but such students were not actively sought. Joe's plan was to be aggressive about recruiting students from all the families of the community. Previously, non-Catholic attendees had been required to participate in Catholic religion classes. Now, Joe suggested that the school offer these students alternate religion classes, not merely acceptable to them, but even formulated especially for them by those responsible for their pastoral care.

Joe took his idea to Bishop Raymond J. Gallagher, and the bishop was interested. Together they contacted the local ministerial association and invited the members to a brunch at Central Catholic High School, where Bishop Gallagher presented the proposal.

The ministers were shown around the school and given information they could share with interested parents, so that all could make considered judgments. The plan was well received by the ministers. A tentative curriculum was to be set up by the school administration showing how it could be worked out.

Nothing further came of the proposal. Perhaps too many people were not yet ready for that kind of outreach.

When Joe had time at home, he continued to work in his shop and to fly the Pietenpol with the Safety Twin Engine installation that had won the Oshkosh award. When he had added the extra engine, it brought the empty weight up to 1,550 lbs. Even with that weight, one afternoon, with only one engine running, he took off, flew it for thirty minutes, and landed. Tests showed he had 240 feet of climb per minute even on that single engine. After installing this configuration in a Cessna, a Piper Tri-Pacer, and the Pietenpol, he judged the latter to have given the best performance.

Although Joe's experimental work still gave him great enjoyment, the Scripture sharing meetings he and Josephine were attending were now a dominant part of their lives. One evening Joe stood in a meeting to tell his Dayton friends how much he loved them.

"If you love us so much, why don't you come with us and help us build a church?" someone shouted. Some of these people were preparing to go spend two weeks helping a small Methodist congregation in Puerto Rico. Joe hesitated, but after some prayer, and with his pastor's approval, he and Josephine decided to go.

It was a blessing to shovel gravel and lay block with those people while Josephine helped the women cook. But that turned out to be the smallest part of the blessing.

As the Halsmers drove to Tampa, Florida, from where they would fly to San Juan, somehow they took a wrong turn and temporarily lost their way. As they prayed, "Father, lead us back on the right path," Jesus gave Joe a vision of Himself. Some fifty feet ahead, on a rise at the side of the road, with one arm outstretched, was Jesus, pointing forward down the road, smiling and looking straight at Joe!

"You are going the right way," He said.

At that moment, they found that they were indeed on the road to Tampa, and the momentary confusion ended.

There was a deeper meaning to it for Joe. At that sight of Jesus, and His reassuring words, Joe knew in his heart that he was doing what God wanted him to do: working with the Methodists, or any other brother or sister who proclaims Jesus as his Lord.

This love for others that was filling Joe's heart began to seek expression within his own family too.

"Dad, when are you gonna get something you can teach us aerobatics in? When are you gonna teach me how to do a snap roll, or a slow roll?" Neil had heard his father talk so often of his barnstorming days and he wanted some of that fun.

Neil was a good pilot. He had flown his dad's pancake twin and considered himself a bona fide test pilot. Now he wanted to learn aerobatic skills. And so did David and Robert, and the older boys when they were around.

In France, Joe found an open-cockpit biplane that had been used for WWII advanced training. The Stampe, with its swept-back wing, was well balanced, easy to maneuver, and had good snap roll characteristics. It needed some repair, but the price was so reasonable, he ended up buying three and Seaboard brought them from France.

When Joe took the first one up, the wind in his face brought back happy memories of days long ago. He taught Neil inverted flight and how to do slow rolls and snap rolls. David and Robert learned too, and they all loved it. It was a replay of Joe's fun forty years earlier when he had first learned to fly. When the girls came home on visits, or when cousins appeared, everyone wanted a ride in the Stampe. Joe enjoyed so much sharing his love for flying with his family. As the other two machines were restored and licensed, they were sold for enough to pay for the family's fun in their own plane.

That same spring, the local chapter of Full Gospel Business Men's Fellowship, International, had arranged for a Catholic priest from

Belmont, Michigan to be the speaker for its regular monthly meeting in Lafayette. Joe had met some of the members of this group in various prayer meetings around town and he knew from them that FGBMFI was an interdenominational organization with chapters in ninety-four nations. The president of the local unit, knowing Joe was Catholic, asked him if he would like to host Fr. Charles Antekier in his home.

Joe was excited! Father Antekier was to be in town for four days and he encouraged the Halsmers to make plans for him to meet with and speak to others in addition to the Full Gospel meeting. So the Halsmers arranged for Fr. Antekier to speak at an afternoon gathering at the Convent of the Precious Blood. And that evening, he would celebrate Mass in the Halsmers' home. They invited all the priests and nuns in the community to come to either meeting. The Sisters Adorers of the Precious Blood greeted Father warmly that afternoon and asked many questions following his talk. The only visitors who appeared were Sister Ralph and Sister Jane Frances, two Vincentian nuns who served as cook and housekeeper for the bishop.

That evening, close to eighty people, mostly friends from Dayton and other prayer groups around the city, crowded into the Halsmers' large living room for Father Antekier's Mass. Those two Vincentians whose interest had been thoroughly aroused in the afternoon meeting were there again, and two priests and two nuns from St. Boniface came.

Father Antekier was a warm, friendly young priest who had a gift for sharing how powerfully God worked in his life. He knew that many present that evening were not Catholic, so as he welcomed everyone, he spoke respectfully of understanding how dearly these other brothers and sisters loved Jesus.

"But," he said, "because of the cracks in the unity among us, I cannot invite other Christians to take communion with the Catholics."

This has always been an uncomfortable matter in interdenominational gatherings. His open acknowledgement of the pain it brought to everyone made it easier to accept his statement of position. So except for Communion, the people participated fully in the Mass, voicing personal repentance, and praising and singing spontaneously and joyfully.

The Halsmers audio taped the celebration, as they often did of talks and songs they thought worth keeping, and that produced a little surprise. It was a warm May evening and the swimming pool, twenty feet outside the open windows, was still filled with the winter's water. The early crop of frogs croaked heartily throughout the service. They were very loud. However, no one noticed until the tape was played, that at the consecration, the most solemn moment of the mass, the loud background of the frog chorus abruptly stopped. On the tape, the quiet was too conspicuous to be missed. As Father proceeded with the sacred prayers of the canon, there was absolutely no background noise. After communion, when the common praise began, the frogs joined in with their singing, quite as loud and continuously as before!

Following Fr. Antekier's visit, Joe became more involved with the Full Gospel Business Men's Fellowship and the local group elected him their president. In addition to these responsibilities, he often spoke at other chapter meetings around the midwest, testifying to God's power in his life. Association with this group extended Joe's opportunities to share his faith and to pray with others.

One Sunday morning, the St. Boniface pastor told Joe that for some time he had been unable to throw off a cold.

"Would you like for me to pray for you, Father?"

Father B. was a man of faith and prayer, but always quiet when Joe spoke of what God had done in his life. Again this time he made no response, so Joe walked on.

Three days later after an evening basketball game, the two men left the school gym together, stopping to lock the door.

"I'm going straight to bed," Father B. sighed. "I am so sick."

"Father, I'll be happy to pray with you if you like... "

Once again there was no response, so Joe went on to his car.

As he drove home, concern for Father's evident misery was on his mind. He had driven half the five-mile distance to his home when suddenly Joe knew God wanted him to return to the rectory and pray with Father.

Close on the heels of that revelation came the dread of going back and waking a man who had said he felt so weak he was going straight to bed. That seemed unwise, but Joe was certain that God wanted him to return and offer once more to pray.

Driving back and waiting for the doorbell to be answered gave Joe plenty of time to imagine all the ways in which his pastor might show his displeasure at being roused. Sure enough, when he opened the door, Father's face registered surprise.

But before he could say anything, Joe's words came spilling out: "Father, God told me to come back, and if we pray together, He will heal you."

Father gave a long quiet look and then said, "Joe, I'm glad you rang my doorbell."

He invited Joe into the small parlor near the door and sank wearily into the nearest chair. Joe placed his hands on the priest's shoulders, and together they prayed for God to heal him of all his discomfort and pain. When the praying was finished, Father B. jumped up and exclaimed, "Praise God, Joe, I"m healed!"

"Praise God, indeed," Joe thought. "He is good. And He wants His children to obey Him. He isn't looking for people who are smarter, or more spiritual, or more gifted than anyone else. He only wants people who are available, who will use the gifts He's given them."

Many people were becoming aware of Joe's availability.

One day a woman came into the airport office and asked for prayer. Her doctor had informed her she had three lumps in her breast. She wanted prayer for healing right away. Johnny and Hank and Hank's wife, Louise, gathered around her with Joe and together they all asked God for healing.

The woman reported later that in a second examination, no lumps were found in the breast.

Later, Louise herself experienced a similar healing. She found a suspicious area in self-examination and when her doctor examined her, he affirmed her finding, and set an appointment for a biopsy.

Naturally upset by his diagnosis, she came straight back out to the airport and asked for prayer. The three brothers prayed for her and when she returned for the biopsy, it wasn't necessary because the lumps could no longer be found.

The children too were more aware of God's love for them.

One evening at bedtime, Dominic came to his dad and said, "Dad, look at my heel. There's a hole in it!"

It was a strange sight. There was no evidence of inflammation and no pain, but there was an indentation in the sole of his heel almost a half inch deep, and about the same diameter.

After Joe placed his hand on him and asked God to heal him, he went to bed. The next day his foot looked perfectly normal.

Joe never knew what God would do next, or how He would do it. Hank and Joe went to pray for a neighbor who had had surgery for prostate cancer and had been told the surgery was unsuccessful in terminating the cancer. That night in his living room, the man shouted at the top of his voice, "God, I know You died for my healing 2,000 years ago, and I'm accepting it right now!"

Another man, while hearing Joe tell this story in a church, was suffering a nagging pain in his shoulder. He focused his mind on Jesus' healing power and said (under his breath, but with his whole heart in it), "Jesus, please heal me. I know You can do it!" And, he told Joe later, his pain disappeared.

Then there was the woman who was in a coma when Josephine and Joe went to pray for her. The floor nurse told them she was dying, and she never stirred while they prayed. They left a small vase of flowers from their yard with a card.

About ten days later, her husband called and apologized for his delay in contacting them. His wife had awakened later that day and asked for food. The next day she sat up and was so strong the doctor let her go home. Later she went to Florida for the winter with her husband.

God showed His power in a very different way when Josephine and Joe went on a Lay Witness weekend with their Dayton friends. (The Lay Witness is a Methodist program in which lay people are given structured opportunities to share their faith.) Where two congregations had tried to unite in a single church, there was ill will and lack of cooperation. But God gave Joe a word to speak to them about their need for repentance of their unforgiveness toward one another. The people realized God cared enough about them to instruct them, and they accepted His word and made overtures to one another. Before the weekend was concluded, there were joyful embraces throughout the congregation.

Time was flying by and the Halsmer family was growing and scattering. In another year, Joe's age would compel him to retire from the airline. He wanted to take Josephine and the children on one more really special trip. He believed God was telling him he should take his family to visit the Holy Land, Israel, the land where Jesus had lived.

The traveling family was smaller now, with David in the Marines and Joann living and working in town. But during spring break, Robert, Maureen, Dominic, Tim, and their parents packed up and flew off to Paris, Rome, and Tel Aviv.

A cab took them to Jerusalem and within an hour of their arrival at the Casa Nova, Joe began a conversation with Father Ignacio Mancini, OFM. While Josephine was getting the children settled, Joe was telling Father about the Baptism of the Holy Spirit and the joy it had brought into his life.

They hadn't talked long before Father Mancini knelt on the floor and said, "I want this baptism."

They prayed, and with tears of joy streaming down his face, Father jumped up and exclaimed, "I've been born again! I've been born again!"

Father Mancini was an Italian who had studied and been ordained in Jerusalem, where he was now the superior of the Casa Nova, a Franciscan inn for pilgrims. He was also rector of the Franciscan Seminary there. (Later, he served as Custos of the Holy Land.)

He was so excited and joyful about his new relationship with Jesus that he wanted to be with the Halsmers constantly. Joe arranged for a car and Father M. took them to all the holy places they wanted to visit, to Cana, Jericho, and Galilee. He celebrated Mass for them in the Church of the Transfiguration on Mt. Tabor. As he read the appropriate Scripture passages at the various spots, tears rolled down his cheeks.

"Joseph," he said, "Jesus has become alive for me!"

Joe invited him to come to America to see the amazing things God was doing, healing people and changing lives.

"Oh, there is no way I could do that," he said sadly. "I have no time, too much work, and no permission from my superiors."

"We'll pray about it, and you'll come!" Joe surprised himself with his certainty.

Only three weeks after they returned home, Fr. Mancini called and said that indeed, he WAS coming. It turned out this year was his twenty-fifth anniversary year in the priesthood and his superiors were happy to give him time to make a trip to America for his celebration. In addition, a travel agent friend provided him with an airline ticket to the states and back, with stops anywhere around the country he wanted to go.

They all enjoyed the week he spent in the Halsmer home. Joe and Josephine took him to the Charismatic Renewal Conference at Notre Dame University and to local prayer meetings they had been attending. He prayed with people of many different denominations, a novel experience for him. At one meeting a prophecy was spoken regarding him: "God will use you to minister to all His children from every denomination." When he returned to Israel, he was appointed director of an Ecumenical Education Center!

As the summer turned into fall, Joe made another effort to respond to his local parish's needs. Adults were being solicited to teach elective classes to the seventh graders in St. Boniface School. So he offered to teach a class on glider building. For one semester, he brought eight boys out to the airport one afternoon every week and taught them some of the basics of aircraft construction.

They learned some other basics too. One day John J. came in saying he had broken his shoulder in football practice. It had been x-rayed and placed in a sling to immobilize it.

"Do you boys believe God can heal John's shoulder?" Joe boldly challenged his students.

These were Catholic boys who had been taught God could do anything. But at the snickering and pinching that went on, Joe knew they weren't sure God had any real interest in them.

"Let's do this right," Joe said. "Gather around John, and lay your hand on his shoulder, or his arm." Joe placed his hand on John's head and prayed for God to heal the broken shoulder.

When the next week's class time rolled around, John showed up without his sling. He told the class the doctor had asked him to return for a second x-ray, to check on the healing. This time the doctor could find no sign of a break!

In March, 1973, Josephine and Joe returned to Israel at Fr. Mancini's invitaton to attend the First Conference on the Holy Spirit. They looked forward to seeing their friend again as well as to attending the conference.

Both events lived up to their expectations, but God had even more in store for Joe. He was beginning to learn what God meant when He said, "For my thoughts are not your thoughts, neither are your ways my ways." (Is.55:8) As Joe had prayed and spent time thinking about God's will for his life, he became more strongly convinced than ever that the aloofness of Christians of different denominations toward one another was a source of deep sorrow to God. Before his death, Jesus prayed to His Father for His disciples: "... that all of them be one, Father,... May they also be in us, SO THAT THE WORLD MAY BELIEVE THAT YOU HAVE SENT ME." (John 17:21)

This simple Gospel message seemed to burn itself into Joe's heart. It was so plain to him: the reason much of the world does NOT believe in Jesus is because His own followers are not truly loving one another.

When the Holy Spirit conference was over, Fr. Mancini wanted to introduce Joe to some of his friends. One was a hermit who had been touched by Jesus and healed of a serious illness when he was a child. Jesus had told him that when he grew up, he was to work toward the healing of Jesus' broken body. A Spaniard, he had become a priest and had come to Israel to live in a cave in the desert to listen more fully to God.

"So this is what a hermit looks like," Joe thought, as he walked toward him across the sand and saw his weatherbeaten face and straggly beard. As Joe neared the man and looked into his eyes, they seemed to shine with a kindness and a sweetness Joe had never experienced before. He brushed aside Joe's outstretched hand and grasped him warmly in a bear hug. It was as though both men had been waiting for this moment for a long time.

Sitting together on the rock at the entrance to his cave, the priest told Joe about himself and his desire to see the divided Body of Christ healed of its disunity. As he finished, he stood, and reaching out, he poked Joe in the ribs and spoke emphatically, "We must turn back to the simple Gospel message!"

Joe was deeply touched. He believed this encounter was God's way of confirming what He had been teaching him. He pondered for a long time over what God had said about people caring for one another and building each other up. He had made clear that the first step in loving another is getting to know that other. Joe recalled how grateful he had been throughout his life for his career as a pilot. He had seen how air transportation had helped the people of the world come to know one another better than ever before. He had always hoped that knowledge would be a contributing factor toward world peace. Now he began to wonder if knowing others is enough. Could people ever really love one another without acknowledging their need for God's help in the matter?

The next day, Father Mancini took Joe to a Carmelite convent. The Mother Superior was a woman who had left a life of wealth in Italy twenty-seven years earlier to enter this cloistered order and spend her life in prayer. She spoke with the two men through the bars of the cloister. They talked about prayer, about seeking God, and about helping others to hear the good news of their salvation. She said that for years, her only spiritual reading was the Bible.

"You know," she said, with emphasis, "for unity in the body of Christ, we must turn back to the simple Gospel message!"

Emotion overwhelmed Joe as he realized God had brought him all the way across the earth to this spot, to confirm for a second time the simple Gospel message He had imbedded in Joe's heart: "Love one another."

CHAPTER 11

CROP-DUSTING AND CHANGE

Seeding with the "miracle" Stearman—
$500 humility lesson—trip to Belize

Joe's sixtieth birthday had sneaked up on him. He had recently passed the same demanding physical examination that had been required every six months over many years to maintain his pilot's license. But now his Air Transport Rating for commercial airline flying would automatically expire because of his age.

He made one trip the first week in January, 1974, and returned on the fifth. The next day, he blew out the candles on his cake and retired from the airline. A short time later, he and Josephine flew to New York to enjoy the company's retirement party for him.

Soon after that, Seaboard did purchase those Boeing 747s. So the advancement into new equipment quickly set him outside the mainstream of that which had been his life for so many years. Some pilots, when they retire, don't know what to do with themselves, but not Joe. He always expected to spend his latter years with his airport, his experimental work, and his Stampe. Now his days were filled with the added excitement of watching what God would do next. And unexpectedly, a return to barnstorming, which gave him such fun years ago, suddenly became a real possibility.

At the licensing of pilots and the registration of planes in the 1930s, the Civil Air Agency had begun to frown on daredevil stunts and flying at low altitudes. Following World War II, the agency took a much stronger stand in an effort to put a safe image on flying. Aviation was

Joe being congratulated at his retirement from airline flying by Henry Heguy, Seaboard executive, in January, 1974.

evolving from fun (or war) into a serious means of transportation. Planes were no longer for joyriding. They were a new way to travel. To lure the general public into accepting this, the aura of excitement and danger had to be replaced with an image of comfort, convenience, and especially, safety.

The barnstormers who outlived their era, deprived of their reckless livelihood, had shifted into a more acceptable role. The highly maneuverable biplanes with the short, reinforced wings, so successful at hauling passengers in and out of small, tree-ringed fields, now with a bin or a tank added for seed, dust, fertilizer, or spray, made excellent cropdusters. The daredevil pilot continued to fly his plane, was better paid, and enjoyed improved status as an agricultural worker.

The Halsmers had done a little crop-dusting in the fifties, but the demand for that service then had been slim and seasonal. As they expanded into other types of flying, they decided that the limited uses of the duster didn't warrant their keeping one on hand.

But farmers of the seventies now had larger investments in their crops, and they were more inclined to spend money on weed or pest control than farmers of the fifties.

Joe knew about a rugged little primary trainer widely used during World War II that was now being flown in agricultural crop control. He persuaded his brothers they should buy a Stearman. Not only would it be fun to fly, but he could make some money with it, now that he would be at the airport full-time. When he located one in Alabama with a 300 HP Lycoming engine, equipped as a sprayer and duster, Joe was excited. The men sent Neil, with his cousins, Tom and Dick, south in the airport truck. The boys had plenty of tools with them because they knew the plane was in poor condition, but it was thought to be flyable. All three boys were good mechanics, and the men trusted their judgment as well as their abilities. When they arrived at their destination, they examined the plane, and the purchase was arranged. They loaded the extra parts, together with a second engine included in the deal, into the truck, and Tom and Dick began driving home. Neil took off in the Stearman.

A couple of times during the day, the boys in the truck called home to learn if Neil had made a trouble call from anywhere. They would go help him if he needed it, but there had been no phone call. When Joe went home for supper, he was becoming concerned. That old Stearman was no racing machine, but he had thought Neil could fly it home in a day.

Joe was to attend a prayer meeting in town that night. Still thinking of Neil, he drove back across the road to the airport to look once more off to the south. It was dusk as he got out of the car and stood listening for the plane, but he saw nothing and heard nothing. He had to be on his way. It was already 6:45 P.M.

Just as the time registered in Joe's mind, he had a strong thought that he should pray for Neil. So he said a brief but sincere plea, "Father, please take care of Neil. Whatever his need is right now, please meet it."

And with deep faith, he thanked God and headed back to the house to get ready for his meeting.

As he finished changing his clothes, Joe heard an engine humming in the distance and coming closer. Again he returned to the airport and, sure enough, the Stearman was landing. He helped Neil tie down the old tail-dragger, but because he was pressed for time, there was not much conversation.

When Joe returned about 10:00 P.M., Neil got up from the sofa where he had been resting, and said, "Dad, did you pray for me at about a quarter to seven this evening?"

"As a matter of fact, Neil, I prayed for you at EXACTLY a quarter to seven! I had looked at my watch." Joe continued, "Why do you ask?"

"Well, Dad, I had been flying all day and wasn't feeling well. About 6:45 I became so nauseated that I thought I was going to have to set it down before I passed out. I was over Frankfort, only twenty miles or so from home, and I wanted badly to make it in. But I felt so rotten that I started to descend and circle, looking for a spot to put it down.

"Then, all of a sudden, I felt okay. The nausea simply left me completely. It was really strange. I pulled up then and came on in. I slept a little here while you were at your meeting and I still feel great."

That plane had to be overhauled, of course, before it could be used in the crop operations. In doing that job, the exhaust system was found to be leaking into the cockpit. No wonder Neil was nauseated. He had breathed a lot of carbon monoxide fumes between Alabama and Indiana.

And there was more. The normal result of exposure to carbon monoxide fumes is a terrible "hangover" headache, but Neil had no headache at all!

Joe went right to work with his new toy, the Stearman. Although seeding by air was nothing new, the Halsmers initiated, at least in their area, the sowing of soybean seed into immature standing wheatfields. They learned that if they sowed the beans into the wheat at the right time, it could give the farmer a second crop on his land in one season.

Joe in his beloved Stearman, "feeding" the foliage of a soybean crop. 1975.

Near the end of May, wheat in Indiana has generally grown to a height of about twelve inches. Sowing beans at this time not only gave the beans an early start, it allowed them to germinate and begin their early growth protected from weeds by the growing wheat. When the wheat was ready for harvest, the young bean plants were small enough to be undisturbed by the combine as it moved through the fields. And the beans still had time to mature and be ready for harvest after the first hard frost.

Many farmers took advantage of this double-cropping technique. There was also a demand for foliar feeding of crops by air, an interesting manner of applying fertilizer to the leaves of the plants instead of to the soil. Joe and his old biplane kept busy.

In the summer of 1977, Joe left the Stearman in the hangar and took Josephine to an ecumenical charismatic gathering held at Arrowhead Stadium in Kansas City. 50,000 Christians from nearly 100 different denominations, ranging from the Pentecostal and Holiness backgrounds through mainline Protestants and Roman Catholics, gathered and worshipped together without denying the differences in their beliefs. Joe came home from Kansas City more convinced than ever that God wanted him to work for the unity of His broken Body, but he wasn't sure how. How much time did God want him to spend with airplanes and his experimental projects? Sometimes he thought he wanted to be completely free of airport responsibilities and devote all his time to helping others. When someone became interested in his Stampe, he sold it. He did know God wanted him to tell the good news to everyone he encountered. And he tried to do that.

A man Joe had known for years was ill with cancer in the hospital in Frankfort. Frank and Joe had flown together years ago, so Joe went to visit him and pray with him. Frank was very sick but he was glad to see his old friend and he listened to his words about Jesus. He invited Jesus into his heart and soon he was released from the hospital.

On Joe's way to the hospital that day, a big semi-trailer had nearly run Joe down. At the time, Joe had seen a face in the truck window that was so horrible it had shaken him up as much as the close escape. After the events in the hospital room, Joe believed that the devil had made a direct attempt on his life to prevent his visit with his friend, Frank. But again, God had protected him.

On another occasion, Joe prayed with a friend in the local hospital and they talked about Jesus' love for everyone.

In a few days when Joe returned, his friend said that his roommate, who had seemed to be sleeping when Joe had been there, had told him he'd heard all that was said about Jesus. The roommate had, for the first time in his life, turned to Jesus in repentance and asked Him to be his Savior.

"Then," the friend told Joe, "last night he died."

Joe was trying to be obedient to God as fully as he knew how.

One night about midnight, he awoke and told Josephine he needed to phone John B.

"It's very late to be calling someone," she cautioned him.

But Joe knew what he had to do. God had awakened him and told him this friend needed $500 and that he should offer it to him.

When the man answered the phone, Joe asked, "John, do you have a problem?"

There was a pause. Then his shaky voice said, "Joe, I sure have. I need $500 desperately. There's nowhere I can get that kind of money. I've been thinking about suicide."

The next morning Joe took the money to him and thanked God that he was able to help others.

Twice Joe prayed with a retired Franciscan priest when he was hospitalized. Both times he regained his strength and got back on his feet.

Another priest friend from the high school suffered a brain tumor and Joe drove to the Indianapolis hospital to see him. He was not allowed into the room, so he stood in the hall and prayed for him. Soon afterward Joe learned he had been released from the hospital and experienced a time of improvement.

At a Full Gospel meeting in Bass Lake, young parents brought a four-year-old girl who had one leg three inches shorter than the other. She walked on her tiptoes on that foot. After Joe and the others prayed for her, she put her heel on the floor and walked normally for the first time in her life.

The child's parents, as well as an uncle and aunt, and two other people who saw what happened, all accepted Jesus into their hearts that night.

Another interesting instance of God's work involved a Christian woman who held prayer meetings in her home for many years.

Joe went to visit Gladys in the hospital when he heard she was dying of cancer. She was weak and didn't respond to his inquiries or prayer.

Her sister, sitting at the bedside, told Joe later that she was alarmed when she heard him tell Gladys, "You'll be sitting up in that bed in three days!"

But when he returned in three days, Gladys WAS sitting up in bed, still weak, but looking cheerful. She wanted to know all that had been going on while she had been comatose. And she had things to tell Joe that she said God had told her.

"God has a healing ministry for you," she said. "He told me to tell you He wants you to fast, and not to be afraid to step out into the deep."

Then, looking Joe right in the eye, she asked, "Tell me, Joe, how long do I have?"

Joe prayed in the Spirit and found himself telling her, "You have only a week. But God has work for you in that time."

Gladys did die a week later. And her sister, who stayed at her bedside throughout, told Joe that in that week, Gladys encouraged two nurses to put their trust in Jesus.

Between prayer meetings and visits to the sick Joe continued to keep his beloved Stearman busy.

Because of the low altitudes flown, agricultural flying is generally acknowledged to be some of the most dangerous flying done. The operator naturally wants to carry the heaviest load of seed or spray he can lift, so there is always a fine balance between carrying that maximum load and being able to get off the ground. In addition, when flying at an altitude of fifty or a hundred feet, there is little recovery time available if something goes wrong. Joe loved the challenge of it.

On one occasion with the usual heavy load, he had to make a tight turn to stay clear of some high lines. In the turn, the stick began to get sloppy, a real danger sign that his speed was too low. He already had full power on, so the only thing to do was lower the nose. The altimeter already showed less than 100 feet. About the time the wheels were hitting the standing wheat, he finally got up enough speed to lift the nose and get out of there. God was there once again!

Then there was the time God gave Joe a short course in humility, and charged him $500.00 for it!

That particular morning Joe had the Stearman loaded with 1,000 pounds of rye seed. He was in the plane with the engine running when he remembered a map he might need. Setting the brakes without cutting the engine, he got out and went back into the office. Returning to the plane with his eyes on the map, Joe crawled into the plane and released the brakes. Beginning to roll, he glanced to the right, and was horrified to see his right wingtip about to brush the tail rotor of a jet helicopter.

"Where the hell did THAT come from?"

In an unusual lapse of caution, Joe had moved his plane without first making sure all was clear ahead. (How quickly in stress did he revert to language that earlier had been so characteristic!) Into his mind flashed a vision of a crumpled tail rotor on a $300,000 aircraft—maybe a torn fuselage—OH, NO!

His reaction was immediate. Throttling back, he jammed hard on the Stearman brakes and paid the price for his carelessness. The tailwheel rose off the ground and the plane tipped up, stopping inches short of the expensive helicopter. The Stearman's wheels were locked in place, but the propeller continued to turn as the engine groaned on. Safe in his cockpit, Joe quickly cut the engine, flinching at every bump as the tips of the prop struck the cement apron, each time curling back the metal tips a little farther. The prop finally stopped about the same time the weight of the load of seed shifted forward. The plane settled heavily on down, coming to rest with its lower cylinders on the cement, the prop mangled beyond repair.

What a blow to a pilot's pride when he stands an airplane on its nose! But Joe had made a deliberate choice. It was him or the helicopter. His plans to seed rye that day were over.

There is a sequel to that story.

Parts for old aircraft are not easy to find. Joe searched his mind for a place to get another prop, finally calling Ponca City, Oklahoma, where the dealer there thought he might have one.

"What do you want for it?" Joe asked.

"$1,500.00." But he came back to the phone and said, "No, I guess it's been sold."

Then Joe tried an airport in Pennsylvania.

This time the voice on the phone said, "Yes, I have a Hamilton Standard prop for a 300 Lycoming engine and I need $500.00 for it."

That sounded like a bargain after getting a $1,500 quote from Oklahoma. Then there was a bonus.

"I have a student here I'm taking out on a cross-country," the man in Pennsylvania said. "If you'll pay for my gas, I'll bring you the prop." Joe couldn't have hoped for more.

But there was more. Later that day, when the man and his student pilot delivered the prop, Joe helped him unload it from his plane, and listened to the story he told.

He ran a flight school for missionary pilots, and like most missionaries, he was chronically short of funds.

That morning he had prayed, "Lord, I need $500.00 today. Please help me." Then Joe had called for his prop.

After Joe heard that story, he felt a little better about bending the Stearman prop. At least his $500.00 helped someone. And he learned a little lesson in humility as he recalled his former lack of sympathy, even scorn, when he had seen others stand a plane on its nose.

In June, 1978, Ray Bullard, the Indiana International Director for Full Gospel Business Men's Fellowship invited Josephine and Joe go to Belize in Central America with him and several other Full Gospel men from South Bend. Ray knew a Fr. Raymond Castillo in Belize, who wanted some lay people to come witness to his parishioners about how God had worked in their lives.

The team was warmly received in Belize City and had comfortable quarters at the Bliss Hotel. The people were friendly and grateful for their coming and they welcomed them into their homes for prayer meetings and Bible studies. The local chapter of the Full Gospel met, with several national dignitaries in attendance, and Joe and the other men ministered there. The men visited the hospital and prayed for many sick persons while Josephine spoke and counseled at a women's Bible study group.

Fr. Castillo pastored a parish in Belmopan, the new capital city, and they were driven the forty miles out there for a meeting of about 200 people. The following evening, back in Belize City, all were invited to say a few words at an evening Mass.

The day before they were to return home, Joe and Josephine sat in the little restaurant in the very center of Belize City. As they looked out the windows, they could see the drawbridge over the Belize River. It intersected the main street, and a large open area on both ends of the bridge accommodated the gathering of many people milling around, all wanting to see who else was there to look around. The CocaCola-furnished sign over the door said, "Mom's Place". Inside, it looked exactly like a set from a Humphrey Bogart movie, with the rough wood flooring, square tables covered with red gingham cloths, and straight-backed wooden chairs.

At the next table, a young French couple had confided they were headed that day, on foot, for the Mayan ruins. Both teachers, they were on a camping tour of North America for the summer.

"Have you ever thought," Joe asked his wife, "how the blessings resulting from some project seem to be directly related to the personal effort required by the project?"

"Like what?" Josephine wondered.

"Well, you know how awful that malaria medicine we're taking makes us feel. And that Mexico City agent at the airport, who insisted we couldn't stay overnight without passports, gave us a bad time, didn't he? It was a good thing we could produce the notarized statement the Indianapolis policeman made for us when he found we'd left our passports at home. After all, we had been told we didn't need passports. And remember the disappointment we felt when we arrived here in Belize and were told that the man who had invited us had gone to the United States? That was before we found that Fr. Costello (pronounced Cos-tay-oh) was not the same man as Fr. Castillo (pronounced Cahs-tee-oh), our host, who was in Belmopan, his hometown.

"The discomforts and negative aspects of our trip have been more than neutralized by the positive things we've experienced," Joe continued.

And together they marveled over the latest demonstrations of love God had given each of them. For Josephine, He provided a visit to the shrine of Mary, Our Lady of Guadalupe. At this site is commemorated the vision of Mary by the Indian, Juan Diego, in 1531 when his serape was imprinted with her picture. It is called miraculous because no study has ever been able to identify the elements of the color on the material or explain how it was applied. In the Halsmers' overnight stay in Mexico City on their way south, Josephine was thrilled to learn that the basilica where the cloak is displayed was near enough for them to make a quick visit there to view the beautiful 461-year-old garment.

Then, not one to play favorites, Jesus fulfilled one of Joe's dreams when, on the day of their arrival in Belize, their hosts took them on a tour of some nearby Mayan Indian ruins. These were places Joe had read about with great interest, but hardly expected to see in his lifetime. These blessings, besides all the healings, reconciliations, and a deliverance had made it a fruitful week.

The next day, the flight back home was uneventful, but on arriving, Joe learned his mother was hospitalized. Within a few days, his Mom was home again, but her hospital stay led to an increased ministry to the sick for Joe. The first day he went in to see her, he recognized in a nearby room a woman he knew, the wife of a Full Gospel member.

"Marty! What's going on? What's wrong with Jim?" Her husband was lying quietly in the bed with his eyes closed.

"Come out into the hall," she pushed Joe ahead of herself. "Jim had a stroke and his whole right side is affected. The doctors say he'll never work again."

And before Joe could make any reply, she added, "But God is going to heal him. I know He is! I know He is!"

"Of course, Marty, of course, God will heal him," Joe encouraged her. And they returned to the room and prayed for Jim, still lying quietly in his bed.

Joe checked with Marty the next day when he went in, and she was quite agitated, although Jim seemed about the same.

She told Joe that the hospital chaplain had been there and she was upset by what he had said.

"Mrs. B., you need to prepare yourself for a changed life. Your husband will probably never regain the use of his right arm. God will help you learn how to compensate for the changes this will bring in both your lives." He was certainly trying to be helpful and encouraging. But he didn't know Marty!

"I told him," Marty said, "don't you DARE say my husband will never use his right arm again! The God I know is going to HEAL my husband!"

And God did heal Jim B.'s paralyzed arm. He returned to his regular employment within a few weeks.

Then there was the butcher. Joe met him in the hall one day and he told Joe he had had surgery for prostate cancer but the doctor had told him they had not been successful in removing it all. The two men prayed and he too claimed God's healing. He went home, had no further symptoms, and later became very active in local politics.

That day after they had finished praying, the butcher said, "Joe, there's a priest in the room down the hall who is very worried and discouraged. Why don't you look in on him?" And he gave Joe the room number.

When Joe entered the room, the man was lying quietly on his bed. His response to Joe's greeting was listless. Joe tried to strike up a little conversation and he learned the priest was from St. Joseph's College in Rensselaer.

As Joe questioned him in a friendly way, he confided, "I had some tests done, and I just know I have cancer." Those were his words, even though he had not yet received the results of the tests.

So Joe said, "Father, may I pray with you?"

"Oh, no," he replied with a hint of surprise in his voice. "I'll be all right."

"What's the matter, Father? Don't you believe in prayer?"

Now that was Holy Spirit boldness!

But that question caused a note of irritation to appear in the priest's response: "Oh well, if you want, we can say the Our Father."

By this time Joe knew the man wanted to be left alone, but he said gently, "Sure, Father, we can say the Our Father. Then when we finish that, I am going to ask God to heal you."

He looked at Joe with more interest than before.

"You sound a little Pentecostal to me," he said.

"Praise the Lord!" Joe replied, and they prayed the Our Father together.

Then Joe laid his hand on the priest's forehead and began to ask God to heal him from the top of his head to the tip of his toes, closing by praising and thanking God for the healing already taking place.

The priest murmured a faint, "Thanks," and Joe left.

When he went back three days later, the priest was gone from his room. At the nurses' station, they told Joe, "Oh, that man from St. Joe's went home. All his tests showed nothing wrong."

CHAPTER 12

THROUGH TURBULENCE TO TRIUMPH

Traumatic decision to sell the airport brought depression and fear—Learning to love, listen, and accept change—The prophesied miracle in the Stearman

When Joe wasn't praying for the sick, he was having fun with his Stearman. Flying in that open cockpit proved to be a satisfactory replacement for the airline flying he had enjoyed for so many years. He was glad to be done with lengthy traveling. The lustre of flying all over the world had dimmed somewhat as his body began to complain about the discomforts of repeated bouts of jet lag. He was now more focused on other things.

From early on, Joe had, at least subconsciously, probably expected one or another of his children to take over the family business. But things had not moved in that direction.

Joe, Jr. had signed on as a pilot with American Airlines, so he was not available. Pete, upon his return from Vietnam, had become a full-time professional race car driver and made his home in California. Neil went to work for a large corporation as an executive pilot. Patrick had entered the Franciscan Order and had lived away from home since he was 13 years old. In 1980 he had been ordained to the priesthood and was stationed in New Mexico.

David had helped in the seeding/spraying operations, but he had reentered Purdue following his time in the Marines, and he wanted to complete his education. Robert also had worked at the airport, but he too was enrolled in Purdue, and busy.

Mark had gone to Honduras with the Peace Corps and was happy there, working with the campesinos.

Marianna, an elementary school teacher, and Joann, a dictrict administrative manager for Wang, were both happily married and living in Chicago and Cleveland, respectively.

Maureen and Dominic were working on postgraduate degrees at Purdue University, she in English literature, and he in aeronautical engineering.

Tim was a high school student. For the moment he seemed to be following in his older brother's footsteps, winning the Central Catholic Grand Prix for go-carts in his senior year.

Although the children had liked growing up near the airport and enjoyed the familiarity with planes, none of them saw themselves devoting seven days a week to the business. That's what the transportation business requires.

Their reluctance to enter the Flying Service was not surprising. The operation of a private business in the '70s and '80s was certainly unlike the opportunities open to Joe and his brothers at the birthing of their airport in the '30s.

There was little incentive in these later years to risk capital in areas of uncertain endeavor; in fact, there was much to inhibit it. The formerly dependable profits from instruction, charter flying, gas sales, and hangar rental were now reduced by restrictive safety regulations, the constant threat of liability lawsuits, and spiraling insurance costs. Maintenance orders still were coming into the shop, but dealing with regulatory agencies was becoming exasperating. Joe's enthusiasm for his business, diminished by the changing business climate, was further shaken after the incident of the Stearman's bent prop.

But there was still work to be done.

Then one day, flying home from a seeding job, he experienced a terrible vibration in the plane. He thought at first maybe the hopper had come loose and was flopping against the fuselage. He was only about 200 feet high, so he spotted a flat field below and landed. He could see immediately that the engine was a mess. A cylinder was pushed off the case and had broken a connecting rod. As he made his way to the fence, a tractor approached and he hailed the driver. It was a friend, and he asked Joe what he could do to help.

"If you'll just take me on your tractor over to your telephone, I'll call my brother to come tow the plane home. I'd appreciate that." Joe was pleased to avoid a long walk for help.

Johnny came over with the tug, and they were able to tow the plane the two miles home over little-traveled back roads.

When they had bought the Stearman, they had set aside the extra engine with hardly a glance. Upon examination, it turned out to be in good condition, so they installed it.

Now what to do?

It was beginning to be evident that Joe, and his brothers as well, were getting weary of the daily chores of operating the airport. Joe wanted to be free to go in to the hospital and pray with someone when they called him. After all, for years, he'd been ready to pump gas whenever a customer appeared. Many a night he had gotten out of bed to flip on the switch for the runway lights when a late client had called to say he was returning from a trip.

But now, his emotions about all this were mixed. He loved his airport, but he preferred to read his Scripture. He had been proud of serving the public well. But now he, John, and Hank all found themselves grumbling about the very things they'd been so happy to do earlier.

Joe loved flying that old biplane and he hated the thought of selling it. But the newly-overhauled engine had increased its value, and right then the market was good. Maybe they ought to see what they could get for it. Maybe they even ought to look into how much they could get for their other planes also. At that time, the kinds of planes they owned were selling well. If prices took a downward turn, then they might wish they had sold. Maybe they ought to get rid of everything connected with the business. They even began to think about selling the airport. The responsibilities they had carried for all these years began to seem so burdensome.

It was hard for Joe to consider all these options, but he knew he had either to shoulder his responsibilities or shed them.

Change is inevitable. As summertimes fly by and the winters roll into the past, as the boys outgrow their pants and the girls get their ears pierced, so too do changes take place in parents.

The turbulent sixties had come and gone with sons and daughters ranging in age from two to twenty-two. While Joey was flying for his country in the Navy, with Pete and Neil in the Army, and David in the Marines, Patrick felt called to make his own statement by filing for conscientious objector status, even though, as a seminarian, he was not subject to the draft.

With Joe's World War II background, he was taken aback by this development. He was proud of the time and effort he had given to his country. At first, the nationwide attack on the "establishment" angered him. Long discussions ensued whenever father and son spent time together and they certainly came to know one another better. Joe began to consider other aspects to which he might have given less thought before. For one thing, he conceded that perhaps his generation had been too apathetic about the elective processes. Maybe if voters had made a greater effort to choose good leaders, they might be getting more responsible representation in their government.

"There must be long and hard thought," Joe began to agree, "before arms are taken up again." He came to be proud of Pat's stand for his beliefs.

Changes were coming so fast, it was hard to stay abreast. The price of gasoline was up. Environmentalists were concerned about the fouling of the atmosphere. Solar energy and doing things the natural way was in.

Joe had always been intrigued by the windmills in Holland. It seemed to him to be a terrible waste to fail to harness wind power. Thinking of a way he could increase the velocity of available wind, he enlisted his brothers' help.

They began to build. Inside a large aluminum venturi tube with a front-end diameter of fifteen feet, they centered a stationary cone pointing forward. Inside the cone they placed a large direct-current generator which developed twelve volts of electricity. Fastened to the generator with a series of pulleys was a shaft mounted on a bearing so it could turn freely.

Welded to this turning shaft, behind the cone, was a large drum on which were butt-welded twenty tapered blades. These were set at an angle which turned the drum as the wind blew. Another set of twenty blades was at the rear end of the drum, with guide vanes to direct the airflow. The air forced through this section was exhausted into the open venturi which, at this point, flared out to a twenty-four-foot diameter. Thus, by combining ram air pressure at the entrance with negative pressure at the rear they managed to increase the velocity of the wind a measured 100%.

After many months of work, to test it, they set it securely on a truck and moved it at varied speeds up and down the runway. Now confident that they had a workable wind machine, they mounted it alongside the hangar on poles. They planned to use the power developed to generate electricity.

Two days later a tornado swept across the woods behind the Halsmer home, uprooting several trees. It made a beeline for the wind machine, lifted it off the poles and tossed it aside, destroyed, before moving on to the southeast. No buildings or planes were damaged.

The machine had tested so beautifully and seemed so well constructed, its loss was a great disappointment to Joe. But now, he regretted all the effort he had spent on it and wondered if the time might have been better spent telling people about Jesus. He couldn't bring himself to

The ill-fated wind-powered electric generator, 1981.

rebuild or restore it.

Meanwhile, the three brothers had found buyers for first this plane and then that one. More and more they talked of getting rid of the airport itself. It seemed there was little to look forward to. Except for their families, flying had been the whole of life for all three of these men. What could the future hold? With all the aircraft gone, there was little to do except mow the grass and, once in a while, gas a transient plane. With no more income from the business, the necessity to make a difficult decision faced them.

Nobody wanted to do it, but it made sense to sell the airport. They listed it with a local realtor and nothing happened. They advertised it nationally and there was no interest. It had been a tough, emotional process to decide to sell it. It was traumatic to see that no one even wanted it.

The local realtor with whom the airport was listed finally called. He had a client who was thinking of setting up a travel service and combining it with charter work. But time passed and no more was heard from him.

Then there was another show of interest. Three local pilots and a mechanic, experienced men, wanted to begin operations. That sounded good to Joe. He hoped to see it remain an airport. Maybe he could retain some use of the runway for personal flying. But these men had little money and their offer was very low.

That week the Halsmer brothers and their wives gathered around Joe's dining room table: Johnny and Betty, Hank and Louise, and Joe and Josephine. (Whatever sum was received would be split three ways.) They had poured their lives into the development of this business. It was depressing to think that it meant so much to them, and was so little valued by others.

The six of them had prayed together before about selling the airport. Now they prayed again: "Lord, what is Your will in this matter? Several years ago we acknowledged You as the head of our business and asked You to lead us. Now again, we ask You for Your guidance." And they assured Him of their trust in His care.

What kind of a counter offer should they make? They knew they needed to get more than had been offered, but on the other hand, no other buyer had put in an appearance. They finally decided on a figure and put a time limitation on the response. They didn't want to be sitting around waiting.

But of course, they were waiting.

"If the sale goes through, what will I do?" Joe wondered.

Josephine had tried to talk to him about planning for his retirement years, and he always said he would never retire.

"You're as young as you feel." That was Joe's watchword.

And he had planned to stay young forever. Now, suddenly, he felt old. He was restless with no airplane to fly, yet he had little energy to pursue his experiments.

Three days after the meeting around the dining table, a phone call came from the realtor. He had a contract that he wanted to bring out for the Halsmers to look over. Unrelated to the earlier discussions, it was an offer to take an option on the airport at a price considerably higher than what they had asked only last week. It was for a term of six months, renewable for another six months if the buyer chose. No other information was available about the buyer's plans.

Again they waited, now with emotions in a turmoil. The potential of a good sale price was heartening, even exciting. But being one step closer to a sale strangely saddened Joe. What would it be like to have the airport no longer a part of his life? What if the buyer used it for something else—closed it down?

The changes coming about in his life were pushing in on Joe. Whether the airport sold at this time or not, he knew he would never again be immersed with Johnny and Hank in the day-to-day business of flying as they had been for so many years.

"Where are You, Lord?"

As Joe spent much time in prayer and sought His face, God had a surprising answer for him. It didn't seem to relate at all to the problems he was having. But he had a clear understanding that he should listen carefully to what others were saying in a conversation. Joe's heart had already become filled with love. Now he understood that a powerful aspect of loving others is to encourage them, and a good way to encourage others is to listen to them.

Much of the time prior to this revelation, when someone was speaking, Joe, immersed in his own thoughts, would often be inwardly forming his own response. (Or his mind might have been light-years away, plotting how to make some mechanism work.)

It sounded like a very difficult change for him to make, but the promised power of the Holy Spirit was there to help. Once Joe realized what he needed to do, it became a challenge to sit quietly with his mouth closed and listen to others speaking.

He came to know a great peace in his heart as he tried to follow this direction. It wasn't easy to walk this path, so different from his lifelong habit of charging ahead, speaking his opinion forcefully, and perhaps intimidating others with strong statements. But each time he spoke too quickly, he was reminded that repentance brought God's instant forgiveness.

God reminded him, also, of something He'd taught him some years earlier when he first began speaking at Full Gospel meetings. Not only does the devil work at dividing Christians, he especially works to divide couples who love one another.

It was a recognizable pattern. As Joe and his wife would get ready to go to a speaking engagement, they would find themselves in a spat about something or other, verbally jabbing at each other. Finally, the two of them realized they were misusing their strong wills against one another instead of building up one another. Joe remembered what he had learned about unity with other people: It doesn't mean we need always to agree with others, but it does mean we must care about them, want the best for them.

The deeply adversarial attitude often present between the forces of management and labor had long disturbed Joe. At the same time he was a member of the Air Line Pilots Association and flying for Seaboard as a union pilot, he was also, as part owner/operator of the flying service, the employer of flight instructors as well as several office and shop helpers. From these perspectives, he had a firsthand look at both sides of the labor-management issues.

"Why do both workers and supervisory personnel," he wondered, "find it so difficult to realize that their goal is a mutual one, prosperity? How much more productive our world could become if we all really tried to respect and listen to each other as individuals."

It was a happy day when the airport option contract was renewed for another six months. But the effect was that the waiting and wondering dragged on. The three brothers had to face the hard fact that the end of their flying business was at hand, regardless of the outcome of the option. So they began to dispose of their tools and equipment. The listing of all these hundreds of items was tiring and time-consuming and required many decisions about what to sell, what to give away, and what to keep. It was especially difficult to apply themselves to such depressing work with the sale still uncertain.

Joe spent more and more time praying and reading his Scripture. He began to realize that when God closes one door, He always opens another one. Things aren't always what they seem to be. Endings can also be beginnings. He had learned a long time ago that, in aviation, things aren't always what they seem. He learned to trust the invisible air to hold his plane up in the sky. And he learned to trust the instruments in his cockpit, instead of his feelings or what he could see, to guide him through the sky.

Can you picture the "crabbing" attitude into which a pilot must place his plane in order to land it in a strong crosswind situation?

If the wind is blowing from, say, his right, he must point the nose of the plane into that wind and aim to the right of the runway in order to compensate for the wind drift as he descends. Only in this way, when he actually touches down on the ground, will he be on the runway itself, and not blown far to the left.

Once, in making a landing at Shannon, even after many years of experience, Joe was almost tricked by his senses.

He was descending through clouds in a very strong crosswind. Knowing all the relevant factors from the instruments, such as his forward speed, the strength of the crosswind, and his rate of descent, he was keeping the plane to a certain speed and attitude. At 200 feet, he broke out of the ceiling, and could see the thirty-degree angle at which he was approaching the runway.

Prior to that moment, Joe knew the drift angle at which he was flying, but only when he could see the ground did the angle of approach appear dangerously oblique. It surprised him so much that he almost overcorrected. Instead, he had to reestablish quickly the heading which had brought him down this far correctly. He had to disregard what his own eyes were telling him.

Indeed, things are not always what they seem. Joe could see it so clearly now: listening to others, especially at times when he wanted so badly for them to listen to him and agree with him, was a special opportunity to love that other person.

Finally, some good news: the long-awaited phone call came from the realtor. The buyer would exercise his option to purchase the airport.

The Halsmers all agreed later they had underestimated God. They had asked Him to take care of the airport sale and while they waited, and wondered, He had it all under control.

Indiana state government officials had worked hard trying to interest industries in locating in the state. One of the sites being considered was land immediately to the south of Halsmer Airport. Now that this place had been chosen, the airport would have to be closed, since an airport legally controls the heights of buildings in its lines of approach. Early in the deliberations, a corporation fronting for the state had optioned the airport in order to hold it available, but these details were unknown to the Halsmers.

Now, even though the sale was supposedly assured, there turned out to be months of uncertainty and delay still ahead.

Meanwhile, the Indiana Regional Full Gospel Convention was scheduled in April and Joe was expecting Josephine to accompany him as she had for several years. However, their daughter in Cleveland had asked her mother to come give her a little help with her infant son.

When Josephine told Joe that she thought she should go to Cleveland instead of being in Indianapolis with him, he was disappointed and unhappy. He wanted his wife with him. But again, God reminded Joe how Paul had written to the Corinthians: "No one should seek his own good, but the good of others." (ICor.10:24)

"Maybe," he thought, "Joann's need for her mother at this time should come ahead of what I want."

So Joe attended the convention alone. And, as usual, the generosity of God was not outdone. Not only did he enjoy himself, but God bolstered his sagging self-esteem in prophecy through the lips of one of the speakers: "You will have every bit of ability you need to do what I want you to do."

Joe returned home after all that prayer with renewed strength and confidence in himself.

Finally the actual sale of the airport was concluded, giving Joe a new impetus into the future. He arranged to have a shop building erected on his home lot and he moved his experimental work into it. He began work on a gyro propulsion design that he believed had possibilities. He spent time working on the wing for his turbo-charged aircar. And he had in mind an improvement for the valve system of an engine that could double the power output.

Then, after the surge of interest brought on by the move into the new shop, thoughts of building things slipped again into the background of Joe's days. Instead he kept busy sharing with others the goodness and faithfulness of God in his life. And he knew people wanted to hear about it, along with his flying adventures, as various groups continued to ask him to speak about his life.

One story he liked to tell was about the evening a group of friends prayed for him at the airport when they learned he would be flying the Stearman the next day.

After the prayer, one of the ladies exclaimed, "Oh, Joe, a picture came into my mind in which Jesus put one of His angels beside you to protect you—and then He gave you a book."

At the time, Joe didn't attach any significance to the book, but he was happy to have the prayers, and an angel beside him.

The next morning he went out with a full load of 1,000 pounds of bean seed to sow.

As he flew to the seeding site, he thought about how good God is. How blessed he'd been to be able to work and earn a good living for his family at something he enjoyed so much.

"Too scared to steal, and too lazy to work," he used to say with a laugh, about his flying career. How else could he explain spending his whole life having so much fun?

Now he could see that God had been overseeing his whole life from the beginning.

"Father, You have guarded me through more than fifty years of flying. You've taken me across the Atlantic more than 1,400 times and the Pacific over 450 times, with never a serious accident or injury of any kind. You've protected me through over 30,000 hours of flying, some of it extremely dangerous. Now, here I am, past seventy, back again in an open-cockpit plane enjoying the wind in my face. What a life! Ah—there's my field."

Joe circled, checking the surroundings thoroughly, looking for electrical or phone wires, trees, or any other obstacle standing higher than its surroundings. At the far end of the field, some trees, buildings, and high-tension wires prevented a good approach, so he would do his sowing from the east.

He made a pass across the field, pulled up sharply, and began a wide turn, preparing to return to the opposite side of the field for another pass. Just below to the left, exactly where he had pulled up, Joe caught a glimpse of sunlight glinting on some wires.

Wires! He could hardly believe his eyes. Wires across there? He had come up through that very spot!

As he flew on and his angle of sight changed, Joe could see why he had not spotted those wires before. They were attached to a corner of the barn at one end. From there, they stretched to a pole, but the pole was hidden by a large tree near it. He had flown right through those wires.

Joe repositioned himself for a safer sweep across the area and completed the job with no problems. As he flew back home, he said a prayer of thanksgiving for the angel that Jesus had put beside him to protect him once more.

As he recalls that story, his mind touches on all the ways in which things are now so different. Across the road from the little house that was new to him and his young family in 1948, the landscape is changed. His childhood home has been torn down, along with the barns and the little milk house where he and his brothers washed so many milk bottles. Gone are the towering black walnut trees, sacrificed to the widened and improved road. Gone from the sky is the familiar hum of the small aircraft, formerly so much a part of the whole area.

The attraction of the sky is different now. As Joe remembers flying his beloved Taperwing or the DC-4s, the Connies, or the stretched eights, he thinks of all the departure times he's met in his life. And he anticipates with joy that last takeoff, when he'll meet the One who chose him to fly and gave him such a wonderful life.

Halsmer Airport, Lafayette, Indiana, 1963

*Are you reading someone else's copy of this book?
Isn't there some pilot or veteran you know who would
enjoy his or her own copy?*

*What about a birthday gift, or Father's Day?
or Christmas? for Dad, or brother? for Grandpa?
or Uncle Jim?*

To order additional copies, fill out the blank below and send to:

THE APPLE TREE PRESS
174 Sand Drive
Naples, FL 33942
(813) 262-3982

PRINT CLEARLY

Name _____

Street _____

City _____ State _____ Zip _____

Please send me

_____copies of CHOSEN TO FLY @ $14.95 $ _____

Shipping and handling   _____

Surface shipping anywhere (2 to 6 weeks delivery), $3.00 **OR**
Priority mail: USA, $4.00; Canada/Mexico, $6.00; Other, $10.00
Call for shipping charges on bulk orders.

Tax (5% for Indiana addresses)   _____

Total $ _____

☐   My check is enclosed.